DEAR M

"VIEWS ROM A WAYWARD CHILD, CONVERT, EX-JARHEAD, BRAZILIAN JIU-JITSU BLACK BELT TO A SON OF MARY

ALEX GOTAY, JR., MA, DMIN

En Route Books and Media, LLC
St. Louis, MO

Make the time

En Route Books and Media, LLC
5705 Rhodes Avenue
St. Louis, MO 63109

Cover credit: Brandon Morel

LCCN: 2020944014
ISBN-13: 978-1-952464-21-8

Dedication

To Momma Mary

Contents

Introduction

Why I wrote this book

I remember right when I got out of the Marine Corps, about 2003 or 2004, I wanted to continue to train in martial arts, Brazilian Jiu Jitsu. I had picked it up while there and knew that it helped me with many aspects of my daily life, so I thought it would be cool to continue.

I searched on the internet, and I finally found a gym somewhat close to me. This was before the UFC, Ultimate Fighting Championship (what some refer to as MMA or Mixed Martial Arts), got big, and there were about 3 schools in all of Houston during this time.

I had to go.

Why? I didn't feel my workout plan was complete. Being fresh out of the Corps, I was so used to rigorous, daily workouts. I was an infantryman, a Rifleman, and all we did was work out, train and clean (of course, but that's for another time). My daily workout took about

3 hours.

I was working for the county at a Boot Camp for young men, and I had to be there at 7am. I would wake up at 3am. I would lift weights for about an hour, run 6 miles and then swim for about 30 minutes...six days a week.

I'm stating all this to show you how in shape I was before I went. I hate to sound corny, but I really was a lean, mean, and really good fighting machine...so I thought.

I remember walking in the gym (we call it a gym, others may call it a dojo or studio). I looked around at all the students. I knew that I could kick everybody's butt in there.

We went through the warm-up as normal. The instructor showed the moves for the day. And then it was my favorite part, time to spar. I remember his looking at me, the instructor at the time, asking if I wanted to train, or should I say spar. He said it looks like you have done this before and are in shape, so I want to make sure that you're okay with training.

Training consists of basically live sparring. For those of you who do not know, I want you to think of a cage match. It's what you guys would call UFC. There's a part in every match where people go to the ground, and what I've noticed through the years is people say they need to stand back up because it looks boring. But to the trained eye, there is a lot going on. There's way more than what meets the eye.

I'm stating this because from the outside it looked like nobody in that room was a match for me. However, I was about to be taught in my very first lesson—do not judge a book by its cover.

The instructor paired me up with somebody who was much older than me. He looked like he was out of shape. He was very big. What I mean by big is very round. The guy sat down and was smiling at me when I walked over to him. I knew I was just going to kill this guy. If you're reading this, please know that I mean that in the most Christian way possible (I'm being sarcastic, of course).

The bell rang, which means it's time to spar.

All I remember was this guy went from a round, out of shape bowl of fun into a spider monkey mixed with Bruce Lee. Within about three minutes, he made me tap, submitting me against my will about four times. Submitting means to bend or choke someone against their will into stopping the match. Just look at a UFC event and the end of one. That's a good idea of what happens every day in our schools. I thought to myself there's no way that this is happening! It happened about two or three more rounds.

The coach paired me with different people who seemed on the outside very different from me. They seemed like they could not handle me and were out of shape.

However, the same thing happened each time. The bell rang, and I got submitted a bunch of times. I remember when everything got done just thinking to myself, "Man, this martial art works! I have to come back because if these people who look like they're out of shape can do this to me, then there's no stopping what somebody like myself who is in shape can do with this martial art thing."

I kept coming back day after day, week after week, month after month. That was several years ago. I learned that Brazilian Jiu Jitsu is not only about looks, but it's also about the work that you put into the art itself. From the outside perspective, it may look weird; in fact, it does look weird. Two people rolling around on the floor making the other submit looks somewhat odd. In fact, to the untrained person, it looks hilarious!

It was odd to me at first. When I'd walk into a room where a fit person is sparring someone who looks out of shape, I would assume the stronger person would win. On the contrary, it's the one who puts a lot of work into the art itself. Why? We have a saying in Brazilian jiu-jitsu, 'Nothing substitutes mat time.'

In other words, you can read a lot about the art; you can even look at videos. Oh, you can even look at the UFC. But, until you actually spend time on the mats training specific moves made for yourself, perfecting the art for your body type, you will never get better. You will never progress in the art.

Why in the world am I starting a book on Mary with a story about an ex Jarhead learning Brazilian jiu-jitsu? Well, just as it took many hard years of Blood Sweat and Tears to grow in the martial art, it takes the same spirit spiritually to grow in holiness and discipline to get into knowing who Mary is.

You see, I'm a convert to the Catholic faith. The idea of Mary was not something that upon my first or even second look was something that I wanted to grow in. She was a foreign concept to me that seemed so far away from the world I lived in. However, sitting with what God gives us and the many different things that have been revealed to us through the years in the church has allowed me to grow and see our mother for who she truly is. A vessel to get to know our Lord even deeper. I know for some of you that sounds so odd, so foreign. I get it. For others, you know who Our Mother is personally. I'm with you, also. This book is for both and all in between.

I think we make holiness so complicated sometimes. We make it harder than what it is. Holiness is simply falling in love with God and letting Him permeate every part of you. It is nothing more than stepping into God's plan for your life. It is perfecting what God has in store for you, and that takes work. It does not happen overnight. And just like BJJ, you can learn about the moves and how to do it, but until you actually do it, you will not really learn the art. In other words, you may know a lot about Mary and holiness but until you actually "perfect your art" or put into practice what you have learned, growth will not happen.

Many of you who are reading this book are just like myself walking into that gym years ago. At first glance, we may have an idea about everything that's going on around us, but only by continual learning do we grow. That's what holiness is, continual growth in the love of God. And just like the martial art Brazilian jiu-jitsu, you will have good days just as much as you will have bad days. It is the same thing for growing in holiness and getting to know Jesus through Mary.

Mary is the perfect example for us as we grow in holiness. The submission of her will to the Father was perfect and effortless. Consider the first day I walked into the BJJ gym. I was submitted against my will. In the end, I had no choice. **Mary's submission was perfect.** It did not take any blood, sweat, or tears (like growing in BJJ). She knew that if she wanted to grow fully in God that her initial response had to be YES! This is something we can all learn from, in that we all need to simply submit and grow.

Mary's perspective of God and her son, Jesus, is very different from ours. After all, she carried, nurtured, and raised our Lord. She was even betrothed to the Holy Spirit. That's a very mystical and deep concept that many of us take for granted.

You may have grown up in the church and may even know a lot about Mary. I think that's amazing and is needed. However, I still think you might get something out of this because the more we sit with Mary the more we come to know who our Lord is and grow in a deeper relationship with Him.

You may be on the opposite side of knowing about Mary. She may be a foreign concept to you. I want you to know that I've been there. It took a long time and much "mat time" for me to arrive where I am with

Mary now. However, I really hope you also sit with this. I hope and pray that you, "Let the words of my mouth, and the meditation of my heart, be acceptable"(Psalm 19:14). In other words, be open to what God wants to show you about holiness and Mary and grow in a deep appreciation for what God has given us in His divine plan!

BUT, before we start we have to start right!

Come Holy Spirit, fill the hearts of your faithful and kindle in them the fire of your love. Send forth your Spirit and they shall be created. And You shall renew the face of the earth.

O, God, who by the light of the Holy Spirit, did instruct the hearts of the faithful, grant that by the same Holy Spirit we may be truly wise and ever enjoy His consolations, Through Christ Our Lord, Amen.

Every day, I start with this prayer. My days are constantly filled with making tough decisions, giving advice, and overall making sure I am reaching out to new people with the Holy Spirit. I cannot give of what I do not have. None of us can. I also do this for you. As you're reading the prayer of the Holy Spirit, the hope is that you let the Holy Spirit guide you in reading the words on the pages to come. More importantly, let these words access the part in all of you that knows God exists. He speaks in different ways.

As a professional Youth Minister and Theology Teacher, trained in Theology and Philosophy (just look at the bio on the back cover when you get a chance), I've realized through the years a lot of us come from different starting points. We all have different foundational points that allow us to view life from a sort of "lens." If you were to combine my life experiences with my formal education, my experience, and my letting the Holy Spirit have access to my inner thoughts and actions, you will find what you come out with is a perspective that is a little different from most. Please do not let that stop you from reading. I am a work in progress just like everyone else! And what you're holding is the result of not only the things I've already stated but also years of Spiritual Direction, trial and error, and letting God do His work through me.

I get to travel all around our great nation and speak to so many different young people (pre-teens, teens, and young adults). This book is written for you.

Before I go any further, I want to make sure that

you "hear" me say this: my approach is a little different. I can say that with conviction because I've been to enough places and realized how different I am.

Okay, but please keep reading. I am not saying that my approach is "bad," "better," etc. Nope, not at all. It is just different, and that's ok. If you knew my personal life, you would understand why.

The booklet you have in your hand is supposed to be as if I'm standing here talking to you. So, some of the things that you see and "hear" are from that perspective. Teens do not like reading for the most part, especially something like this. I try my hardest to just speak from my heart. I try to do away with the "big words" that usually are found in books such as this.

I also want you to know that I truly do believe that the Holy Spirit can speak to us in many different things, especially culture. I am in the process of writing a book for the more "theologically inclined" on culture and how to use it. If it is not published by the time this is, please be on the lookout and add it to your prayers.

Back to what I was saying, in the book I draw heavily from Vatican II, the Catechism of the Catholic Church, and the Scriptures. They all state pretty much the same thing…make sure you're using the "culture" of the people you're speaking to in order to connect them to our faith so that they might grow from it. We all learn better from people who talk like us and think like us because we can relate to them. This is no different. Of course, I'm paraphrasing.

However, take a look at this,

> "Furthermore, theologians...are invited to seek continually for more suitable ways of communicating doctrine to the men of their times...In pastoral care, sufficient use must be made not only of theological principles, but also of the findings of the secular sciences, especially of psychology and sociology, so that the faithful may be brought to a more adequate and mature life of faith" (Gaudium et Spes, 3, 62).

There are obviously way more teachings that reflect this. What all of these documents and teachings show are simple. We are to connect the dots to something familiar to those you're speaking to. Again, I am speaking to teens and young adults using their "culture" here in America to speak about something and someone that is very important to us, our faith and Mary.

So, before you start, say a prayer for me and my

family. I really do have a feeling this is the first of many short booklets about Mary, Our Mommy, that I will write. I've been praying for you…. Let's do this!

Chapter One
God's Plan in HIS-tory

Drake, "God's Plan"

I'm a firm advocate of the idea that God speaks in many different ways. He is the ultimate Creator, especially in all art and not just "fine art." God can and does use art to speak truth. If you're someone like me, raised in the hip hop culture, you see how certain words and phrases can speak truth.

About 2 or 3 years ago, a song came out. I was giving a conference. I decided to throw certain parts of the track into my talks. I would find ALL teens and young adults sing it on cue! When I mean ALL, I mean ALL. From Indian, to Asian, Hispanic, African American, the LifeTeen, etc. Every type of parish and teen would cue in. The track is "God's Plan" by Drake. If you haven't heard of this song, then you probably have been living under a rock. You may find it on YouTube at https://youtu.be/xpVfcZ0ZcFM and you will see. Back to the track…Cue the beat – the artist's girl asks if he loves her, and he replies, "Only partly," explaining he loves his bed and his momma. He adds, sorry.

The entire track is about how things both good and bad, even people plotting against Drake, even the good things (which shows we need to pray for Drake. LOL- I'm half joking) somehow work out for God's plan. In the Letter to the Romans (8:28), St. Paul writes a letter, a sort of email (in today's world), that reminds the listeners what life is all about. He states, "We know that in everything God works for good, with those who love him, who are called according to his purpose."

Did you catch that ALL things, both good and bad, work together for "God's Plan." If we stop and look at our lives, we can resonate with the words from the Prophet Drake—oops, I meant Drake and St. Paul. God writes straight lines with crooked paths. It's so true. I wouldn't be here if that weren't true. I think it's true for a lot of us. However, for purposes of this book, I want to focus on that one line by Drake, "I only love my…my momma."

Even Drake, who is not speaking of specific things about faith, knows that from the beginning, in his life, love for his mother stands true. It's probably because the great love she has shown for him through the years. The second part of Romans 8:28 states, "…with those who love him." What greater love does a mother have for her son?

Applying this to Mary, if all things work for good for "those who love him [the "him" is Jesus]," then everything she does works for good! Better than good because the end of her love is Jesus, our Lord! If you stop and think that's how a good mother's love is, you know it's sacrificial. It doesn't have to boast. It doesn't have to get the credit. It simply bears the pain (for example Childbirth) of her child and does what's best. That is like Mary. That is Mary. Her love is so great and caring that she gave Our Lord His humanity, and saw Him die for you and for me. It must have crushed her. She still did it. And all of it was according to "God's plan." (Cue Drake Voice)

What I mean by God's plan is not the song, but rather all through scripture. God's plan is salvation history. It is God's story. It is our story. When we separate our story from God's story, we miss the best part of God and what He has given us from the beginning. In this case, it is Mary. She's "there" from the beginning if you stop and look. She is a part of God's plan. So, let's turn to His plan. His plan in salvation.

God's Plan in Salvation History

The Beginning

Let's take a look at God's plan in the beginning. Genesis 2 talks of God's creating everything, and it was good! On day 7, God created man. He breathed life into man from dirt (v. 7). That breath is the Spirit of God. We can say it is the Holy Spirit. The Holy Spirit is seen in Genesis 1 also, over everything and helping in creation. We can even say the Spirit helps in redemption.

I don't want to go too much into it, but this is about Mary, so where do we see Mary and the Holy Spirit…uhhhhh, the Annunciation. If I'm speaking a foreign language to you. The Annunciation is Luke 1:31. The Spirit helps in creation. He also helps in the redemption of the world. The Spirit is "alive and active" and helps us each form who we are. If we stop and notice. For instances of this book, you can see that this same Spirit helped in Creation also helps in creating Our Lord, through Mary. Keep reading…

Everything was PERFECT at the beginning of

Genesis 2. Adam works, and loves it! However, he has a sort of moment that I think all of us at some time feel. He is doing God's will by working in the garden. He is doing what he was called to do. He was in perfect communion with God but still is missing something. God waits till Adam notices that he doesn't have a "helper as his partner"(v. 20). He doesn't have someone to carry out God's will and plan for his life. Notice that please, Adam still needs something. In this case, God shows how to perfectly love.

God causes the man to fall into a "deep sleep." It is a very heavy sleep, but it's more than that. It is a place in which God gives revelation. It is a sort of a "state of being." It's more than simply Adam's taking a nap. This word "torper" (deep sleep) is when God reveals something important to those who are "asleep." Check out Adam in Genesis 15:12, Job in Job 4:13 and in the book of Isaiah 29:10.

In all of them, God causes this "sleep" and then reveals or tells them something that will change not only themselves but also the world. They will "see" something that is beyond what they normally see, something that will stretch them beyond the norm. I'm stating all this for a reason, and you will see…just keep reading.

Let's keep going—in Genesis 3:23, the word "man" in Hebrew is "ish." This directly translates to "man" or "mankind." In Genesis 3:16—the word in Hebrew is aw-*dawm*. We use the word "adam" to denote this. It can be translated to "human being" or "human kind." If you notice the words are interchangeable.

Let's focus on Genesis 2:23—"ish." You will see why in a second. God granted him a woman from his side. Her name is Isha (woman). Notice the language. That's no accident. Out of "ish" comes "isha." Out of "man" comes "wo-man." It is a completion of the other. It is a co-acting thing.

At first look, he must have been taken back. He breaks into a Hebrew song and says,

Gen 23-
"This at last is bone of my bones
and flesh of my flesh;
she shall be called Woman,
because she was taken out of Man."

It's beautiful. The Church Fathers state that *woman* came from *man* because they were equal. If God chose the woman to come from the head, that would mean that woman would be above man. If she was taken from the foot that would mean *woman* is beneath him. No, God does something that speaks volumes to our culture about women and men, and theologically He pours out something valuable for Adam and Eve. By being made from the rib that is somewhat in the middle, God shows that man and woman are made to walk side-by-side. Of course, this is speaking to marriage and the bond of mutual love between man and woman.

However, I want to look at it differently. I think this is also pointing to something in the future in the Bible world. Out of woman comes man. Out of Mary comes Jesus. Jesus' role is to save. What is Mary's role? I think you get where I'm going with this…Man and woman are made to co-everything…. Especially in the case of Mary. Mary has always been a part of God's plan.

The Fall

In Genesis, everything is good, really good! It is perfect. Man and woman are in the Garden, not clothed, translation—their birthday suits. Yea, read it. It's there. They probably looked great; original sin had not happened yet. They were eating everything organic. And then something happens. "The Fall" in Genesis 3.

Eve (issha) eats from the forbidden tree. This is where all sin comes in. Theologians call this "original sin." I call this "original ratchetness." This is where WE all have that little thing inside of us that tells us to completely throw out everything and "sin." For all those that do not speak "religion," throw out everything and just be… "ratchet" (insert a Cardi B okurrrrr here).

However. God has a plan for humanity.

Let's paint the scene. Eve and Adam are there hiding in the bushes. They just did the one thing God told them not to. So, they hide. God is walking through the garden and He calls out to man (Gen 3:9)—"Where are you?"

Ok, let's stop for a second. God is all knowing. He is all powerful. He knows what we're going to do before we even do it because He is "outside" of time. He created time. In other words, He knows what's up! He knows the answer to the question He just asked. So, then why would He ask?

I think we're sort of reading it wrong. Instead of "where are you little Adam?" (In the most loving Father voice you can imagine—I'm exaggerating, of course). Think about how we would say in today's culture, "Where do you stand?" He's asking him to sort of see where Adam's heart is at. Guys, we call this a gut check. This is when the coach looks at you after doing the dumbest play and says, "Where are you?" = "Do you stand with us or them?" I hope that makes sense. I'm saying this because I think this is something God asks all of us, daily. "Where are you ____?" fill in your name. "Where do you stand?" "Where is your heart?" or if you're from the neighborhood, "Waddup! You down?!?!" (insert a Shaquille O'Neal voice).

Adam eventually admits his fault, but he really blames it on Eve (Gen 3:12). They (Adam, Eve, and the enemy) are standing there, having done something they weren't supposed to, and are waiting for God's response. By this time, they were dressed, probably high quality stuff since it was all organic and they were in their finest greens. (that's a joke)

God's first response is to the Enemy and how it will be on its belly (v. 14). He then states something we should take a look at.

Genesis 3:15-
I will put enmity between you and the woman,
and between your seed and her seed;
he shall bruise your head,
and you shall bruise his heel"

Ok. I want to focus on something. It is the "....he shall bruise your heel..." The Vulgate translation of Genesis 3:15, or what is traditionally called "the protoevangelium" (first Gospel, on account of its being the first "good news" of the Savior to come) states, "*She* shall crush thy head and thou shalt lie in wait for *her* heel." I remember coming across that years ago. I thought how in the world did this happen. Well...

The translation change was first done by a St. Jerome in the fourth century. He was sent to live in the Holy Land and study in order to translate the scriptures. Living in the late fourth and early fifth centuries, St. Jerome had the extant Hebrew and Syrian codices before him as he did his translating. He was a master of the inspired languages, Greek and Hebrew. Some call him the greatest translator and student of languages in the Latin world. He would know, if not from examining the variant codices in existence in his time, then from the rabbis themselves who taught him, that the Hebrew pronoun in this text needed a feminine gender. Although he actually preferred, at first, to give the verse a masculine pronoun, he ended up choosing otherwise because the feminine "she shall crush" was the more common acceptance among the Latin fathers.

In the East, Saint Ephrem, the Syrian doctor, who knew Hebrew (his native tongue, Syriac, was very close to Aramaic), also gave the couplet a feminine translation.

So, why is "she" so important?

How?

First, how do we read the Bible?

The Catechism of the Catholic Church (CCC) section 115 states that there are "…two senses of Scripture: the literal and the spiritual, the latter being subdivided into the allegorical, moral and anagogical." Ok, that's big words for something I realized years before becoming Catholic. When we read scripture, we take the words on the page as actually historical, really there and for what the words are (I'm trying to make it simpler). When Jesus spoke in the New Testament, there was an actual guy whose name was Jesus. He lived, and he spoke. This is the literal meaning. The spiritual part is different.

The spiritual part is the part, I feel, that we grow the most from. We look at stories and ask questions. How does this relate to God? How does this story show who God is? Who Jesus is? And what does that mean in my personal life? Again, I'm trying to make it a lot easier than the big words do. When I say what it means to me, I mean how it applies to me. For example, if I was going to take the Prodigal Son and look at the spiritual, more specifically the "moral" sense of how to read the story (moral sense is a sub-category of spiritual), I would ask whether I am "living" like the son who left? Am I the Prodigal Son? And does my life look like the Son who ran home to be with his father. This is a Spiritual interpretation of the story. This a "moral" way.

As we shall show in a little while, the "She" (Eve) makes sense when you look at the allegorical, a sub-category of spiritual.

CCC 117 uses the example of the "Red Sea is a sign or type of Christ's victory and also Christian baptism." St. Paul states something profound in Romans 5:12-21. He is stating that Jesus is the new Adam. Jesus corrects what Adam messes up. "For if many died through one man's trespass [Adam], much more have the grace of God and the free gift in the grace of that one man Jesus Christ abounded for many." Jesus is foretold in Genesis 3:15 when God speaks to Adam about what will happen in the future. Scholars call this the Protoevangelion. It is the first good news. It is that God will provide a way, through a man.

Wait? What does this have to do with Mary. Well,

if a way of translating the Bible was done by St. Paul (we call it spiritual/allegory), then it's good enough for us. Go back to the beginning. If man and woman were created to be equal, created to help each other, created to bring about all of creation to serve God, but mess it up…TOGETHER: what would make the way that God saves the world any different…together? In other words, if Jesus is the new Adam, then Mary is the new Eve. She is "there" in the beginning. She has always been there in the plan if you stop and think. She has even been in the plan of my life.

Mary in my life, God's Plan

Holy Nun-Chucks

Mary has been a part of God's plan in my life. I didn't grow up in a religious household at all. In fact, we were far from it. We didn't go to church much. If we did, it was really my mother taking us maybe once or twice a year to a Non-Denominational Christian Church. If I went at all it was with my Titi's and other family. My parents were very young when they had us (I'll speak about one of the reasons why later in the book). A lot of my immediate childhood was spent at both of my abuelas' houses. However, Romans 8:28, "We know that in everything God works for good with those who love him, who are called according to his purpose." Mary was always in the background subtly, and this I believe was a part of God's plan.

When I was a child, I would spend time with both of my grandparents a lot. One lived by Fort Hood, TX, in a trailer and other in Brooklyn, NY, in the projects of Bedford-Stuyvesant. I often tell people I had the best of both worlds, city and country, growing up. My grandmother in Texas used to have a long rope with little beads attached to it, and at the end of it there was this cross with the guy on it. That's really what I thought at the time. It was a rosary. I didn't know what it was, or the power of it. My sister and I used to fight a lot. She would hit me with a slipper, and I would hit her with the rosary. I used to love Bruce Lee as a child, so I would pretend that the rosary was a nun-chuck. I saw rosaries laying all around the trailer like decorations, but I didn't know what they were used for. I knew they had something to do with religious things, but that's about it. I didn't know that this had anything to do with Mary or anything along those lines. I just thought it was decoration.

During that same time of my life, I also spent a lot

of time with my grandmother in New York. Remember, she lived in Brooklyn, NY. She lived on the ninth floor of the projects of Lafayette Gardens. My parents would send me there different times of the year. I remember one year it was raining outside and stormy. I just watched one of those good American movies. You know those movies that make you feel good to be American. Those movies that really move your heart. Movies such as a Nightmare on Elm Street, the Exorcist, Friday the 13th, you know something like that. I hope you see the sarcasm. I grew up watching scary movies. One day, I had just watched a scary movie and my abuela was walking around the house with that same thing in her hands. She was reciting something that sounded like this "Santa Maria, Madre de Dios..." There's more to it, my grandmother used to drink a lot of coffee. If you know anything about Puerto Rican coffee, you know how strong it is. It is called Bustello, and if you're ever running short on gas you can put this inside your car and it will run for about four years. It's that strong... Again, I hope you see I'm being sarcastic.

My grandmother used to drink so much of this coffee, all the time, that her hands would shake if she wasn't drinking. It affected her so much that her hands and her voice would shake. On top of this, my grandmother is from Puerto Rico. When she speaks Spanish, she speaks it really fast. She would be walking around saying what I now know was the rosary, but she would be speaking really fast…

Oh, I left out one part. She would be doing all of this while smoking a cigar. I remember as a kid asking her why she smoked cigars inside the house. Her response to me was that she did this so that the evil spirits would not come. Now mind you, I did not grow up in any faith. The only thing that I really knew about faith was things that I saw on TV. I just told you I watched a lot of scary movies. So, to say that I was scared is an understatement.

My grandmother would say the rosary really fast, smoking a cigar in the back room attached to the long dark hallway. Outside the wind was beating really, really long and hard, and the bars that were supposed to be for safety that were never closed would sway in the wind, and they would hit the wall really hard. I could hear the wind rush. She would close the door at the end of the hallway, and because of her cigar, I could see the smoke coming out from the bottom door rise where she was. And I could see her shadow walking back-and-forth while saying "Santa Maria, Maria de Dios." Picture what that seemed like to me as a child…I really thought that abuela was sacrificing chickens back there. I'm half joking, of course.

Years later, whenever I was on my way to converting to the Catholic faith. I realized that that was a rosary and they were praying it. In my search to know more about the Bible and how it pertains to Catholicism, my first study, while I was a non-Catholic Christian, was on Mary and the rosary. I actually began praying the rosary before I converted to the Catholic faith. I know that part of my conversion is because of those prayers of those two women who used to look after me, and I had no idea what that thing was. I would like to say that they were praying for me. I would like to say that they were praying for my family, who needed it so much during that time. I believe deep down in my heart and all of this is true and that their prayers guided me to see The Catholic Church in a different perspective. This is the power of Mary. She's there in the beginning, if you stop and look.

If you're reading this, stop and write down your first memory of Mary, of the rosary. How have you grown since then? Has Mary been an active part of your prayer life and your life as a whole? Never forget that she is a mother who loves her children, even when we reject her and her son. She "rights" Eve's "wrongs" by simply being what she was/is called to be, a mother who loves from the beginning, and that is according to "God's Plan" (cue Drake voice, ok this time Morgan Freeman. He should be the narrator of my life, btw….)

Back to the Beginning

Jesus is the "new Adam." Where Adam fell short and sinned, Jesus made up for it. Jesus atoned for it. All the things that Adam did wrong, by God's becoming man, He rectified and changed all of it into what is right.

You can see this with other people in the Old Testament. For example, Moses leads his people out of captivity. Jesus leads his people out of spiritual slavery. Noah gives us a promise with the rainbow. Jesus gives us himself as the promise. If you look at the different characters in the Old Testament, you can do this over and over…even with Mary.

If Jesus is the new Adam, then Mary is the new Eve. The plan was from the beginning for man and woman to participate in redemption. We already took a look at that. We noticed that Mary was prefigured. Just like Jesus was to Adam, Mary is to Eve. Eve is the mother of all biological life. Mary is the mother of all spiritual life by giving birth to Jesus.

Sarah, who was Abraham's wife, was seen as faith filled with generous hospitality. Mary is the same. She was seen to be generous in her visit to Elizabeth (Lk 1: 39-45). Rebekah was a virgin (Gen 24:26). Mary is the Blessed Virgin. Again, you can keep going. Mary is "there" if you have the heart of faith to see.

This is the character of God. He always provides. He gives us an opportunity to see his plan in the Old and New Testament. But, it's deeper than that. God just does not only want us to "see," He wants us to act. He provides ways for all of us to find in the lives of those we read about in the Scriptures individuals we come to know and, ultimately, want to strive to be like. Jesus is our goal, and Mary is a deep perspective about Jesus and salvation because God gave her to us to go to, to ask, to communicate with. She wants what's best for us, and it's been that way since the beginning.

Chapter Two

Watch Your Words

Tupac, "Dear Mama"

Through the years, people have come to me for advice when they're going through rough times. All types of people: priests, nuns, moms, fathers, teens, etc. I usually tell them something like this, "When I was a teenager, I used to love this poet. A quote I love from one of his poems goes, 'after the darkest night comes the lightest day.'" It's so true. Look at a tornado in a small town. When you see it on the news, it's dark, it's ugly. There's snow, or hail. It's scary. But the very next day the sun is out and it is beautiful. The sky is so blue. Everything is magnified. Once I came across that poetic line about the lightest day coming after the darkest night, whenever I saw tornados on the news I would think about the next beautiful day. It's like even nature shows this truth.

Whenever I quote that line to people in trouble, every one of them responds with something positive.

"Wow. That's so beautiful." Or, "thanks be God." Again, this tells me how profound the line is. After reciting that line, one very holy priest friend of mine said, "I think I've heard of him." I quickly changed the topic because I knew he hadn't. The line was from the great poet, Tupac. For those who do not know, Tupac was a rapper in the 90's. He was considered one of the greatest in that field of all time. If it would help, look him up. Sidenote—if you do not think Tupac is a poet, you might want to do some research. His poetry is taught in colleges across the nation. There are even classes on his poetry and life. Tupac was more than a rapper. I believe if he were still alive, he would be huge in social justice issues. If you listen to his music, really listen, you will see why I say that.

Tupac has always been a source of hope for me. I grew up very differently (which is a topic for another book), and we did not know faith. In fact, to my father the idea of faith was a foreign concept. And because of that, he did not talk about God at all. I can only recall maybe a handful of times my whole life that he would go to church. To this day now, you cannot say anything about church or faith. He will get angry and shrug you off. Because of the way I grew up and some of the things I already mentioned, I've always had deep questions

about life. I really did not know they were questions at
the time. I thought certain things about life and just
took for granted that these things were normal. They
were not. I had a lot of bad happen to me through my
childhood to teen years that left me questioning a lot.
Tupac sort of spoke truth to me. I know that may sound
weird or odd. But, if you knew me you would
understand why. He did speak and get me to think
about truth and deep meanings of life.

I struggled a lot in my youth. I remember there
were moments of deep despair and I would hear Pac
tell me, "everyday's a struggle, gotta roll on." Or "keep
ya head up." I really felt that. It helped me. It even
"ministered" to me in a way. It spoke to me on many
different levels. His words helped me through some
dark times in my life. I'm sure I'm not the only one. I've
talked to many people, both old and young, who have
said the same thing about his music, about his art. His
messages were and still are relevant.

I think all of us can relate to something or someone
in the way that I am trying to paint Tupac's effect on
me. We all find words from people—random people—
which have a lasting effect on us. One of the deepest
songs (for many reasons) that spoke to me as a teenager
was "Dear Mama," available on YouTube at

https://youtu.be/Mb1ZvUDvLDY - check it –the artist tells his mother there's no way he can pay her back, but he does want to show his appreciation of her.

The entire track expresses his love for his mother, even when times were bad. For various reasons, this spoke to me and still does to this day. I understand that the words that we use every day are very powerful, especially words we use toward our loved ones. In this case, his words expressed how he felt about his mother. Many years after, when he was older, he wrote something to show others that he had a deep respect and admiration for his mother. This is powerful and something WE can all learn from. The words we use to express how we feel and love are precious and have a powerful effect on people... especially when writing these words to our loved ones.

I can apply this line to my spiritual mother, Mary: "But my plan is to show you that I understand." I have to do this in words, and if we stop and think about it, all relationships hinge on words. Sometimes these words are very good. We all love that! However, when we grow in relationships, we have to sometimes learn to use our words more carefully.

Words Make it or Break it

Words are vitally important. Think about it for a second: as I'm writing this you get a meaning from the words being used. Or, think about how good it feels to have your Pops or Moms tell you how proud they are of you. Or, when a friend tells you that you look fresh, or beautiful (if you're a female), today. By the way, you ever notice that when females haven't seen each other in a while, their voices get automatically high? Like really high? Then they start complimenting each other. It's like, "OMG, Becca, I haven't seen you in forever!" (in a high Valley-Girl pitch, insert girl emoji with her hand up)...and then comes the little weird hug where the back foot comes off the ground. Haha. I'm joking, of course. I cannot believe that I probably seen this too many times in my life (#youthministerprobz). If you laughed, it's because you can picture it, also. Ok, that's enough. I'm joking, and you get the point.

I'm stating all this to show how words can affect all of us. They can even hurt. Think of social media and the ugly comments that are made on it. It's sad. I would like to say that "sticks and stones may break my bones but words can never hurt me." Right? That was good when we were children, but is it true? Of course not.

Words hurt. Really hurt. If you think about it even more closely, how deep the hurt is depends on the level of the relationship. A mean comment on social media hurts. A comment from the one you love hurts even more. Just think of a parent or a loved one in a fight. The words being used hurt, and they sometimes even break up families for years. Again, the relationship and depth between the one being spoken to and the one doing the speaking matter. It matters so much that it has lasting effects. This also matters with God. The words you use, when you're in a deep relationship with Him, matter. Ask Mary…

Different Language?

My Sundays were different than most inside of the Christian and Catholic circles. We didn't go to Mass or Christian service. Growing up, I did two things on Sundays: I played basketball, and I got my haircut. This was the norm. Even when my father was away (which was often), this is what I would always do. I would wake up, go play basketball (or ball for us who grew up this way) with my boys (by boys, I mean crew, squad, my day ones, woes, whatever you call your friends) at different parks, get my haircut, and then prepare for the week.

When I got married, I kept the same routine... Until about the first year.

I was newly married to my wife, my queen, my heart, the love of my life, Jessica or Jess (that's what I call her). I have to diverge a second. I'm really not trying to be funny here. She is all of those and more to me. I actually love her with every part of me. I do consider her a gift from God and the Holy Spirit in my household for a number of reasons. Maybe in other books I will explain. I just want you to know she is really the love of my life.

Ok, back to the story—on Sundays, she wanted to go to her mother's house. I quickly learned that on Sundays they didn't do anything I did growing up. They would go to their mother's house and spend time together with family. So, me, being a newlywed, knew every aspect of married life (now I am being funny). I decided I would compromise with her. I would go with her to her mother's, thereby meeting her needs, and then leave after about an hour and go play basketball with my friends. This was me being a good husband. After all, I was doing everything required: loving her... and me! Lol.

The first Sunday visit to my wife's family, when I

thought it was time to leave, I quietly kissed my queen and decided to leave quietly out the side door. My friends were playing down the road. The plan was that I would play a few games, meet her at home, and then get a haircut. I was married. The sun was shining. It was nice outside. Which, by the way, is not normal in Houston. It is usually 95 degrees....with 100 percent humidity. It's hot. I mean really hot and humid. I've seen mosquitos come inside my house and open my refrigerator, get some cold water, then ask me if I wanted something to drink because they're so hot. In short, the eighth circle of Dante's *Inferno*. It is hot as, pardon the expression, hell... at least the wall of fire in the *Purgatorio*. Read Dante in order to get the joke. I think you get it. It's usually really hot and sticky.

I left quietly out the door, and then I heard the door open right behind me. I heard a soft voice that began with, "Mijo, can I talk to you?" from my mother-in-law. Now, if you're Latino, you know what that means... usually a slipper flying at you at the speed of light, or a hand slapping the pigment off your skin. I'm half joking here. What I'm trying to get you to see is that usually when this happens, something "not good" is going to happen. I knew this. So, I immediately thought, "How in the world could someone tell me what to do? I am a man and someone who knows what is going on. I am a father, I'm grown, and I even pay taxes. How DARE someone tell me something about leaving????"

So, I turned around and responded like any real man would, who grew up fighting, kicked out of school, gangsta rap listening, and generally labeled a bad guy. I responded, "Yes, ma'am. May I help you?" I was actually very respectful, to be honest. I noticed that my mother-in-law closed the door behind her. She had her hand clasped, and she exhaled. On her face was an expression that I now know was of a parent who loves her child a lot, but that child just let her down.

She began to tell me that Sundays are made for families and that if I'm going to be a man, I need to realize what is going on and serve my family first. I had no idea what she was talking about. I responded with "yes, ma'am." I calmly but resentfully walked back inside. However, when I got my chance later on, I left quickly out the back door. I ran to my car, hit the music on, and went to play ball!

I remember the day was a good day. I even had a good game. I was married, had a good game, and it was even a beautiful day. I remember driving home where I would meet my wife and thinking this was the best day

I had in a while. I paid no attention to what my mother-in-law stated. She didn't know anything. I knew everything, and my wife and I were good. God is good. It felt good to be American. LOL.

I arrived home, and I knew that I would have dinner waiting because that's what marriage is about.... Please excuse my ignorance. I opened the door to our apartment and remember the air changed from nice outside to freezing cold inside. As I slowly opened the door, I said something like, "Hey, how you doing?" Her response was, "I'm fine." She had an expression on her face that I only know now but had no clue of then. Me, not knowing anything, responded with something like, "yeahhh, girl, I know you are fine!" I even walked up to her and tried to hug her like nothing was wrong (yeah, that was dumb). Let's just say that was not the best way to respond!

Stop. If you're reading, and you're a young man, I'm about to help you more than you will ever know! I'm about to give you a gift that took many years for me to learn, that communication with females is much different from communication with males. In layman terms, the way you talk to your boys/squad/day ones/friends is much different from the way you talk with your girl/bae/queen/girlfriend, especially if you're serious about her. I am sure every married person reading this book already knows exactly what I'm referring to. Again, if you're a young man you might want to get out a highlighter, take a picture, frame this part, even get it tattooed on your forehead....Ok, that was much. Sorry. But you get the picture.

Communication with females is different. See, when a woman says "I'm fine," it's a totally different language than in guy language. Let me explain, as men, as a whole, we are a lot simpler. See, when we are asked a question, we simply state what we mean in a simple statement or word.

Example one:

Hey bro, "how's the game?"
Male Responder: "it's good"

Translation: The game is good. It doesn't mean it's bad. It doesn't mean it's horrible. I really mean, good. Ya know why? Because it is good. That's it. No more. No less. It's good. You don't have to look it up. You don't have to check the tense. You don't even have to know the person who's answering. The response, "good" means....good.

Example two:

> Hey man, "Whats up?"
> Male Responder, "Nothing."

Translation: Nothing is going on. Nothing. You know why? Because nothing is going on, and that's what it means, Nothing.

I'm stating this because female language is much different. (If you're a young man and not married you're going to thank me for this.) I feel that in about 6th or 7th grade, there's a secret land that God brings all the females to, and one of the lessons they learn is communication. It's kind of like Narnia but without the animals and...guys. They learn things like when they haven't seen each other in a long time that they should use a certain high pitch in their voice, body language, and even smile regardless of how they feel (if you don't know what I'm referring too, look back at the example given earlier). They learn how to decorate, how to accessorize... think, they even teach them different colors patterns (like instead of purple, it's lavender, lilac, periwinkle?), etc. What's really funny is I just turned to my wife and asked her for another name for purple. She literally gave me five names that I've never heard of. Some of them I already named. Yeah, she was a visitor of this land.

They even learn how to post things on social media and how to respond to each other's posts (please look at the different heart emoji variations and smiley faces). They are taught a lot on these excursions.

They even learn how to "speak a different language." They learn to say things like "I'm fine," when they really mean, "There's so much messed up with you that I don't even know what to say (and you're lucky that I don't have a *chancla* (slipper), or I would throw it at you)." See, I've been married 20 years now, and I've learned the in-depth intricacies of the female language. I'm a professional now. Call me Dr. Alex "female translator language guy" Gotay. (Hey, if you're reading this, I'm joking of course. I'm being sarcastic, really sarcastic. It's a spiritual gift of mine. Lol. No, I'm in no way saying these things are exclusive to females. So, please do not take this out of context.) Now, back to the story.

I looked at her and I responded with something rude like, "You are ridiculous." Yeah, that was not smart at all. Things got worse, and we obviously got into a fight (yeah, if you're a teen or young person, that happens regardless of what Disney implicitly tells you.

Marriage is not the end of the story; it is the beginning of a new chapter.). It was a big fight—all because of the words that we used and yes, I began it. There, I admitted it.

The words we use mean something, especially when we are in a relationship with the other. Side note- We fixed it obviously. Life has changed and our communication has changed. This is what families do - out of love. I learned that day that communication with those with whom you are in a relationship is vitally important and can change everything. This, in a way, is communion with the other.

Communion

On a deeper level, this is why God gave us the Eucharist (i.e., Communion) so that we might be able to communicate with and be with Him in an intimate way. The longer we walk with God, the stronger our relationship is with Him. We even begin to communicate more effectively with Him. But that process comes with a lot of trial and error, and that's ok. The spiritual journey is not overnight. It is long, and, through it, comes better communication. Our words and actions are a result of that relationship. It begins with the initial response to God.

At the heart of this relationship is communion. At the heart of it is God meeting us where we are and drawing us deeper and deeper into His presence. This is the Christian journey. This is at the heart of the Eucharist. For us and the gospel writers, we express it in actions and words. The actions and words we use show what we believe; they even show how much we really trust in the one we are speaking about. This is at the heart of the gospels, to show who we are and why we must believe in Jesus. Each has a perspective and uses words to paint a picture of why we might choose the Lord and all that He has revealed. Each of the Gospel writers learned to pick their words carefully and show their perspective carefully. Why? Because they grew in their relationship with God. This helped form their perspective. The Gospel of Luke is a perfect example of this. He shows a different perspective. His words will help us each explain and grow in our relationship with God, through Mary. Let's look.

Luke's Words

Categories

How many of you like Netflix, YouTube, Disney, etc? Everyone? Bro, I love it! Have you ever noticed that there are soooo many options?! My wife sometimes can't even pick a movie or show because she says there are too many! Sometimes I get overwhelmed. I open up Netflix and start looking for something and spend 20 minutes just looking! I know it's only me, right? Haha. Sureee. Sometimes, on Netflix or Hulu, I will go to the categories section. It's there that I can narrow things down... Well, the Gospels are a lot like the category section.

See, if you like Documentaries, then you'll really enjoy the book of Matthew. It begins with facts, with all the "baby-daddy" stuff. LOL. Translation: it begins with generations of family history. If you look closely at those families, it's like a soap opera! But, that's for a different book.

If you like the category of Action flicks, then you'll really like the Gospel of Mark. It's short. It flows from Jesus' actions to Jesus' actions - it even skips Christmas. It goes straight to older Jesus with hair on his chest, smelling like Old Spice, after He gets baptized, of course. Ha. I'm joking again. Mark is short and moves really fast. There are parts in it that say, and show, God's actions in the world, really fast.

If you love Love stories, commonly known   as "chick flicks" or romance shows, then you will love the Gospel of John. It is the book that says, "For God so LOVED the world…" It is all about love. (I really hope by now you realize I'm joking)

Ok, if you love investigative stories; stories that have facts, actions, drama, all of it, then you'll love the Gospel of Luke! The Gospel of Luke has everything. The author, Luke, also wrote the Acts of the Apostles. Some say, he walked around with St. Paul. His gospel is the longest of the four gospels and includes the most healing stories, showing his interest in and compassion for the sick. His gospel also has the most detailed birth account and a more descriptive death and resurrection account for Jesus. The Gospel of Luke and the Book of Acts total 52 chapters, making Luke the author of 1/3 of the New Testament, just like St. Paul. In 2 Timothy 4, St. Paul tells us that Luke alone remains with him. This last part is one of the MAIN reasons I love St. Luke's gospel!

Think about it. If Luke talked to the Apostles, the

actual people who walked around with Jesus—the ones who saw, ate, and even "did life" with Jesus—he would obviously have a different perspective than we do. But it's deeper than that: the apostles did not just walk around alone. We read in John 19:26-27 that Mary was given to one of the apostles to care for. Sooooo, that would mean he sat with Mary, also! By the way, I did not make this up. I'm not that smart. This is what tradition teaches us in the Catholic faith. That Luke sat with Mary. This is one of the explanations for a phrase that is all throughout the text, "..she hid all these things in her heart" (Luke 2, 12, etc.). That would make sense because Luke would have sat at the foot of Our Lady, Jesus' mother, telling him about Jesus walking, crying, not wanting to take a bath. Which must've been frustrating because Jesus could walk on water. LOL. He came to know about Jesus' life through the eyes of Mary! Her words, and the Apostles', but especially those things "that she hid in her heart." Made Jesus more "real," more "close" to him. So much so, he even wrote 1/3 of the New Testament about Jesus' life.

Words in relationships have results. They cause us to feel and move. They cause our lives to change sometimes. This is how we are as humans. We hear and react to what we hear. Sometimes, it's good. And sometimes, it's bad. Luke heard a lot and therefore his actions showed a lot. He wrote and lived. Luke's perspective was framed by the words that he heard and some of those are from Mary. He intentionally sought out the community to learn about Jesus through Mary. Do we do that? Do we, at all costs, learn about our faith to grow in a deep understanding—not just knowledge for the head, but knowledge for the heart? Luke was a physician who knew that words are powerful, especially in relationships. This is why he searched, found, and then even wrote.

You?

What is your life "writing"? Ephesians 2:10 speaks of each of us being, "God's masterpiece." Some translations have, "God's workmanship." The root of that word in Greek is *poema*, or poem. You are God's poem. Your life is art, painting everyday with the words you say and the actions you do. What is your life saying? For someone like Luke, sitting with Mary helped form not only how he saw Jesus but also how he lived his life. His art spoke volumes.

Luke's art almost says, "Dear Momma." It is a reflection of sitting with Mary, taking her words in, and letting those words come to life. Sit with Mary and watch her change and deepen your relationship with her Son, Jesus. Of course, Jesus would not get mad at this. In fact, He would honor it because you're honoring His mother. No different than if I sat with my wife's mother, which I love doing, and talked to her about my wife. If I ever ask her to help me, I guarantee my wife will, and does love it. She loves it because she loves her mother and me. She would not be jealous at all. It's the exact opposite. She knows that it's not a competition. Mary knows it's not a competition. Jesus knows it's not a competition. It's about sharing and growing in love for Jesus. It's about knowing Him more deeply by knowing the one who gave him human life.

Today, if you're still reading this, stop. Remember, words are important. So, say the words, "Come Holy Spirit." Then start asking God to reveal who Mary really was and is. Sit with it for a while. Picture baby Jesus, running and laughing. Picture raising him. It's different. That's how Mary saw it.

Often, we only talk about the dogmas, what we believe about Mary, without explaining who Mary is. Mary is more than the mother of God. She was only that because of her relationship with God and with Jesus. It all started with words, out of her relationship with God. Her "yes" should be our "yes." Her openness to the Holy Spirit should be ours. Her words, or should I say word, changed everything. It magnified her relationship with God.

Fiat

"In the sixth month, the angel Gabriel was sent from God to a city of Galilee named Nazareth, to a virgin betrothed to a man whose name was Joseph, of the house of David; and the virgin's name was Mary. And he came to her and said, "Hail, full of grace, the Lord is with you!" (Luke 1:26-29)

Notice the greeting "hail full of grace." Nowhere in the Bible do angels greet someone like that. Look it up. Let's paint the picture with our words. This angel, a being who knows how salvation will come to be and who is acting in perfect accord with God's will and plan for it, says this to a little 13- or 14-year-old, Middle Eastern girl, upon whom Salvation's plan depends. Why? To follow God's plan. This celestial being stops what it's doing and visits a mere little girl, and instead of starting with, "God sent me," it starts with, "Hail full of grace."

Check out the first part, "hail." This is powerful.

Check out what the Catechism of the Catholic Church states, "the greeting of the angel Gabriel opens this prayer. It is God himself who, through his angel as intermediary, greets Mary."(2676) In other words, it's God who's really saying "hail." Why in the world would God greet a mere little girl like that? Maybe because of how God sees her. God knows her and what she will do. God greets her by acknowledging who she will become and what she will do, rather than who she was before His visit. God greets her like this, through the mediator: the angel, to let her know how much He loves her. This is how God works. He loves her that much. What's funny is that, in a way, that's really how He feels about all of us.

God calls us his children for a reason. It is not because of what we have done in the past and our past shortcomings. He calls us children because he loves us. He knows that each of us has the potential to change our lives and change the world. Even if we don't, He still loves us. This is how God works. He is love (1 John 4), and love is always giving. He names us children not because of what we do or will do, but because of his love for us. Sit with that. A perfect example of this is Mary.

Let's keep going.

God, through the angel, states, "...full of grace."

CCC 1996 - "…Grace is favor, the free and undeserved help that God gives us to…[be]…partakers of the divine nature..." Did you catch that? Divine nature. God is divine nature, and his grace lets us become supernaturally more like him. The more we get to know Him and His plan, the more we get to "be" like Him.

What I mean is simple. I have a son (who is just like me). By the way: pray for him/them (I have 2). Each, regardless of how old, how small or tall, how sick, or what color they are, their nature is shared by my helping give them life. But this may not be such a good thing. Lol. However, if we do that as humans, with our mere human nature, how much more does God do that? He does, by grace. I heard Thomas Aquinas say that God is grace. So, in other words, God gives us Himself. In Mary's case, she is "FULL of grace." She is overflowing with it and wants her children to experience it. All good mothers want their children to experience grace, especially Mary. This is one of the reasons why the next part of the story happens.

This celestial being is speaking for God and says, "The Holy Spirit will come upon you, and the power of the Most High will overshadow you." (v. 34)

The word in greek for "overshadow" is *episkiasei* or *episkiazo*, which means "to envelope, or to invest with preternatural influence." In a way, it means to fully embrace the thing. This is really deep because St. Luke is drawing our attention to something that we usually breeze over. He is sort of stating that Mary is the same as the ark of the covenant in the Old Testament.

If you recall the Israelites left captivity in Exodus. God walked before them and would meet with them. They were instructed to build an ark that was sacred, very sacred. God was *very* specific with how he made the ark. Just check out Exodus 25-30. It was holy and reverent because this is where God would dwell (Ex 25:8).

God overshadowed his people. He covered them as they walked through the desert (Nm 10:34; Dt 33:12; Ps 91:4). This was the same cloud that hovered, enveloped the ark of the covenant (Ex 40). Only the priests were allowed to touch it. When the ark was completed, the glory cloud of the Lord (the Shekinah Glory) covered the tent of meeting, and the glory of the Lord filled the tabernacle (Ex 40:34-35; Nm 9:18, 22). The verb for "to cover" or "to overshadow" and the metaphor of a cloud are used in the Bible to represent the presence and glory of God.

I know, that's deeeeeep Biblical Theology. All of that was to show that Luke knew what he was doing.

God knew what He was doing. The angel, God, set Mary up for a home run. All she had to do was respond, and she does, "Behold, I am the handmaid of the Lord; let it be done to me according to your word." (Luke 1:38). Her "yes" sent salvation history into play. Her "yes" allowed for the Holy Spirit to move through her life and in a way set the tone for all Christians. Her "yes" was to the Holy Spirit. Her "yes" allowed for her will to be perfectly in tune with God's plan. Her "yes" allowed God to move mightily. Words have power. Mary's words did. So do ours.

Personal Challenge

Our Yes to the Spirit

In a way, our words allow God's Spirit to move in our lives. Not identically like Mary's, but almost like hers. She freely gave herself to God's ultimate plan, and that is no different than any of us. Her "yes" to the Holy Spirit should be our same "yes."

I have a question, "Do you have a relationship with the Holy Spirit?" I know that sounds weird to some of you. But do you? Remember the Holy Spirit is a Person. It's difficult, I think, because you have God: the Father,

The Son, and "the dove." Right…that's hard. But, our own Creed and teachings show that the Spirit is a Person. When we say a human is a person we mean a body/soul composite. So, it is possible for us to picture Jesus, and the Father, as something like a human father, but hard to picture the Holy Spirit.

So, do you pray and have a relationship with the Holy Spirit? If you do, awesome! Keep moving in the Spirit. If you do not, I want you to stop reading this and go ask for the Holy Spirit to "overshadow" you. Ask the Spirit to show up mightily. God does not do anything with us, we do not let him. A lot of how He speaks is through His Spirit. The Spirit wants to move mightily in your life if you let the Spirit. Go ask. I think you'll be surprised with what you might find in your own life and especially in how you look at Mary.

Mary was full of the Spirit. So much so that Jesus was produced. Her love for God allowed her to be connected in a special way. Pray about it. Pray about it some more. Her "yes" allows us to say "you are appreciated, Dear Momma."

Chapter Three
"Inside and Bold"

Lauryn Hill, "The Miseducation of Lauryn Hill"

There are few powerful women in hip hop culture that can stand up to someone like Lauryn Hill. She took home five GRAMMY Awards for "The Miseducation of Lauryn Hill" at the 41st GRAMMY Awards, including Album Of The Year, Best R&B Album, Best New Artist, Best R&B Song, and Best Female R&B Vocal Performance. That's all great, and I'm sure that's what most remember her for, but not me. I knew she was great when she was with the Fugees. Her powerful voice, rhyme pattern, and way of being stood out to me more than other female emcees prior to this. Take a look at one of her most powerful tracks, available on YouTube at https://youtu.be/9iqxJK6gSlE. The artist says she hears a great many cry for help while searching outside of themselves and realizes that the strength she's speaking about is within her.

I hope you see why her words spoke and still speak to me. The track expresses the need of this world and how there is an inner strength inside of her that she has to tap into. One of the things I love most about hip hop is it's honest and raw. Even if you do not like it, you have to admit that it speaks a reality that many know of. I honestly believe why so many are drawn to it. I've talked to so many teens through the years and all of them, regardless of race, ethnicity, etc., for the most part, love hip hop for the same reason. Sidenote-The days of placing hip hop only with poor minorities is really over and has been for a long time. If you knew anything about fashion and pop culture, not just in America but the world, as a whole you would notice it all around with every group of teens and young adults in the US, for the most part. I dare you to study it.

If you know me and my story, you would know why I've noticed this and why artists like Lauryn Hill resonate with me. She looked around and searched for meaning and purpose and did not find it in the outside world, which made her look in. Her confidence came from searching and finding nothing in the world around her but emptiness and chaos and drawing to the source of true worth. Life happenings simply made her deeply introspect about who she was and what would propel her forward. She arrived at the truth we should seriously think about. She realized that she is not the answer, but God is. Her reality lead her to God. Her truth is to look inside and recognize that true strength depends on the Creator of all, God. We need to recognize that this world is fleeting, as Ecclesiastes 1 states, and it causes someone like Lauryn Hill to look inside and that takes strength. It takes even more strength to recognize that they do not have the answers, and there is something bigger than them. This is God.

It's powerful to be able to look around and notice that things do not make sense and then to be able to self-reflect. This should lead us to question; to ask eternal questions that have been raised for years prior to this time. It's something we all should do and will end up doing at some point in our lives. This world has a way of making us all "look inside." But there's more to it than that. If we solely depend on ourselves for the answers, then we become the sole bearers of truth and everything else and will miss eternity.

Soul

Let me put it a different way. Eternity is a reality

whether we realize it or not. In stating that, it is important to know we are creatures who at one time did not exist; however, we have eternal souls, so once we begin to exist, we continue to exist for all eternity. The soul is immortal, which is part of eternity. Eternity in the sense that there is no time; there is no beginning. The big word we use for this is "aeviternal." It simply means that we are created, just like things in time or "temporal," but we also are everlasting, like eternity. I hope I didn't lose you. You see the part in us, the soul also needs and wants to be united to something bigger than what is right in front of us, than what this world has to offer. This leads to questions, deep questions, eternal questions that demand eternal answers.

If you really stop and think about it, without quenching our souls, we become the end of all things. The answer to these eternal questions will get an answer that solely ends with us as the answer, and eternity simply doesn't matter. We give non-eternal answers to eternal questions. There has to be an eternal answer to all the eternal questions that people have asked through all generations.

Let me tell you about one of my favorite people of all time. He used to ask tough questions. The world around him made him also self-reflect. Let me introduce one of my favorite saints of all time, St. Augustine.

A Saint, Looking Within...

If you're not Catholic and do not know what the word saint means in our Church, then an easy way to understand it is that a saint is anyone who has faith and tries to live it (Romans 1:7; 1 Cor 1:2; Colossians 1:2, etc.). In our Church, a saint is both that and someone whom the Catholic Church has recognized has lived his or her Christian faith to the fullest. The Church does an investigation to check the person's life and then decides if that person's faith is more than a show. A good modern example I'm sure you've heard of is Mother Teresa.

If you're a non-Catholic Christian, you may have heard of St. Augustine, like I did even before I became Catholic. He wrote one of my favorite books of all time, outside of the Bible, called *The Confessions*. In the book he describes his life and all his shortcomings. The writing is very eloquent, very concrete yet not improper. He was a trained orator prior to becoming a Christian/Catholic. Think of one of his professions as a speaker at court. In those days, everything that was done in Northern Africa (again, another reason why I love him) was done by oration (speaking) to the powers that be, and he was REALLY good at speaking! When he became Christian/Catholic he used those same skills to promote the faith. People would come from all around to hear him preach. He was about 30-40 when he wrote his spiritual autobiography and he was REAL with it. He didn't pull any punches. He told on himself. He was honest—brutally honest. I think this is why I love him so much.

He also explains how he looked for things in this world, such as money, fame, etc., but they all fell short of truly satisfying him. He looked to the outside world and didn't find peace. His friends were converting. His mother was pressuring him to convert. After a string of events, he finally gave in. The way he did it was different, though. It was much like Lauryn Hill. Lauryn Hill looks in. St. Augustine looks in. They both look within themselves to find answers to what's going on in the world around them. St. Augustine has a quote that shows how he realized God is within and the source of all strength: *"Our hearts are restless, O God, until they rest in you."*

This famous quote shows that the restlessness of life finds its answer in God. Augustine shows that everything in this world is fleeting and the true strength is finding what God has placed inside you. I call this the Holy Spirit. Lauryn Hill's story shows that this world and the culture we find ourselves in leads to eternal problems, and it makes her look for peace within where she finds God as the answer. So does St. Augustine. He looks on the inside and finds those deep eternal questions that life brings about and realizes that he is not the answer to what life brings. The real answer is God. This sets him on fire!

By looking in, Augustine finds the strength of God to do what God has placed in his heart. This leads to many years of defending and explaining answers to life's tough questions. It allows him to first convert to the Catholic faith and then carry out the mission God has for him. All this was done by looking inward, just like Lauryn Hill.

All great people all start from the same place—they look within themselves and what they find changes their trajectory of their lives. They find confidence. People of faith are no different, other than what they ground their confidence in. And what's amazing is that we can learn supernatural insight from what they "see." Mary is no different. In fact, we can learn even more about God and ourselves by observing what Momma

Mary finds, especially from the perspective of Luke.

Luke and Mary's Introspection

The investigator, Luke, who, by sitting at the foot of Mary, grew in his love and knowledge of Jesus, writes something beautiful. Mary is with the child Jesus and goes to visit her also-pregnant cousin Elizabeth in Luke 1. It is there that Jesus' cousin, John the Baptist, leaps for joy (Luke 1:44). This is proof that the Spirit is alive and active.

Can you imagine the scene? Mary, wearing her bata and in her chancletas wobbles over to Elizabeth, also in her chancletas and bata-which is normal wear for Latinos, who is also pregnant and the baby inside her womb starts to leap. The baby starts to dance, with no music! Then John starts to dance, with no music! This is a party! The hebrew is "skirtao" which means to jump! So, little John the Baptist starts jumping and dancing for joy once he is in Jesus/God's presence! Now that is a baby shower! The baby jumps, music starts, gifts come out, and everyone starts playing the baby shower games (like dirty diaper). The men start playing dominoes....

Wait, I just went to a Puerto Rican or Dominican

baby shower…my bad. LOL. Sorry I was getting into it.

Seriously, What I'm saying is that we can learn something from this. When you're in God's presence, how do you act? Right, I'm not talking about Mass, I'm talking about when you are walking in an average day. Do you "leap?" Do you show joy? Think about it… Pray about it. John jumped, and dare I say he was excited. He was moving around, showing joy because he was in the presence of God! That's amazing. But the question is, Do ours? Do we get excited when we see Jesus? Do we get excited when we know we are about to be in his presence, whether in Mass or in Adoration or prayer, etc. Food for thought….

Let's keep going. Right after the "Baby Shower" (I'm joking of course). Right after the leap, the Bible tells us that Mary responds with a sort of Hebrew poem (v.46-48),

"My soul magnifies the Lord,
and my spirit rejoices in God my Savior,
For he has regarded the low estate of his handmaiden.
For behold, henceforth all generations will call me blessed."

She looks in. She explains how her spirit rejoices

(again, a party!). Her spirit is full of joy and love. Her spirit is connected to God in a unique way that allows her to say something that, taken out of context, can be boastful. She proclaims that "…all generations will call me blessed."

I think this is one of the reasons why I love the Bible and good hip hop (notice I say good hip hop. By good I mean the transcendental properties - which is a book for another time)—they both are so real and honest. They speak from the heart and to the heart. They are authentic and genuine even if it sounds boastful. Taking Mary's words out of context to some might show she is boasting too, but she is NOT! She looks on the inside of her, and she realizes that true power is found in God and that power leads to real strength of life in the Spirit!

Think about it. She is a 13- or 14-year-old Middle Eastern girl who says that "all generations…" - not "some" but "all." Wow! That's realistic and really, really… faithful. Mary is giving us something we should think about and apply to our daily lives if we are going to be true disciples of Christ and look within! She is so humble that she can say that. She is so connected to the Holy Spirit that she can say that.

Life in the Spirit allows your boldness to come from

God. In other words, when you look in you see that God is the answer. His Spirit gives us life! His Spirit encourages us! It lets us know who we are and whose we are. This is living in the life of the Spirit. This is Mary! She is so in tune with God's will that she cannot only speak out that bold statement, but she can also say it with confidence because she KNOWS it to be true. She knows that confidence comes from the Spirit, and this is the principle I want to focus on.

I asked prior to this: Do you have a relationship with the Holy Spirit? If the answer is Yes, then the next part is, "Do you have the confidence in hearing and knowing what the Spirit is asking you to do?" This is a basic Christian calling. It's something we rarely talk about. Are you comfortable with knowing where God has called you?

Answer

Answering this question is deeper than what we may think. The Catechism states it this way:

"...a catechesis of the Holy Spirit, the interior Master of life according to Christ, a gentle guest and friend who inspires, guides, corrects and strengthens this life." (CCC 1697)

Did you catch that?

Life in the Spirit "guides and corrects and strengthens." Notice that it "strengthens," not weakens, you. First, let's put it this way. Let's say you do something contrary to what you know God's will is, so, in other words, you sin. If at any point you feel that you don't belong at Church, or you don't belong with God, that is not the Spirit. Please be careful of condemnation and unbelief. "...he who does not believe will be condemned." (CCC183). A way of looking at unbelief is the turning away from God. It is the thing that pushes you away from God. That spirit of unbelief is the thing that makes you feel that not only are you unworthy but that you do not belong. It pushes you away from all that is good in the fullness of God's view. I've seen this far too often with God's people. This makes us weak.

The Spirit "strengthens" us by affirming we are children of God first. It lets us know that even though we mess up, even though we fall short, we still belong to the Family of God. So, instead of pushing you away from God's house, the Spirit will give you a sort of "healthy conviction" of what you did while making sure you go home to receive the love of your heavenly

Father and Mother! This is what the Sacraments are for, especially if you're Catholic. You have heard the power they have, especially in Reconciliation. It is no longer the priest, or merely wine and bread but actually Jesus in both. It's beautiful! It's God meeting us right where we are because he knows us best. He knows we need something material or physical (bread, wine, person) to grow. For those who aren't Catholic please look up what we really believe about the Sacraments! It will move you! It did for me. For all, the more you spend time with the Spirit (in the Sacraments in a special way, the scriptures, in prayer, etc.) the stronger you grow and the more "bold" you become in knowing who you are and what God has in store for you.

Strength is something we need in today's culture. This is something we read right now. As I am editing this book, I am under quarantine because of the Corona Virus. We do not have it, but New York state is under quarantine, California, Dallas, Seattle, etc. There is a pandemic going on right now here in America. The future is uncertain. But our God is certain. He does not change, and in order to grow and have the true right perspective we need strength. We need strength from the Spirit. If you are reading this, you know exactly what I am referring to. Life without the Spirit to calm us, to soothe us, to let us know that he has us in the palm of his hand is hard. These are the times we need to lean into the Spirit more and more. I hope you understand that.

It's not only with calamities but America is under a big change in spite of the pandemic. There are countless statistics of people walking away from their Catholic faith. To summarize, relatively 60-80% of teens walk away from their faith after receiving Confirmation. Truthfully, I feel they walk away before then. We need young people to stand and "fight" for their faith. That means, doing what is right, in love, always.

Let's make this practical to the world that we are used to living in. When you walk into your lunchroom at school, do you see people who are sitting alone, getting picked on, and who need to feel the love of Christ? I remember a story of a young girl at a high school who would eat her lunch in the restroom crying because she would get picked on and no one would talk to her. Imagine if someone would have not just one day, but every day, did their best to help this young girl at lunch? What could've happened? We all know what could've happened! A change in the girl. What's funny is this is common. In fact, this is a "light" story. If you've been around youth and lived like I have, you know of plenty stories that show how all need help, all need Christ and his love. The love and light of Christ is needed every day both inside and outside of the visible walls of the church.

In Need

I was speaking in a huge city to a group of teens and a very nice parish years ago.. In the talk, I brought up some pretty heavy subject matter (depression, suicide, etc.). I said it and kept on with the talk. I could tell in the middle of the talk that something was going on in those that were present. I made the points that we all need help and that there is a plague going on in the world around us in the form of depression and suicide, but there's hope in Christ! I've seen other Catholic speakers do it. It was no different. I said it and moved on. However, this time was different. I can tell the audience paying extra attention, if that's even possible. If you have spoken to a large number of people in a crowd, you know what I'm talking about. It was dead silent, and I could feel everyone leaning to hear more.

After the talk, I could tell the people who brought me were all talking. They asked me to join them. I walked over. They told me that they recognized I brought up depression and other things. By the way, I have to add that I normally do not bring these things up by far. It was not even in my notes for the talk. It was simply something I felt should be said.

They told me that the week prior they found a young adult in the chapel where Exposition was happening who tried to commit suicide. (Exposition is where we place the Eucharist, Christ we consume in Communion, in a Monstrance—a special object where we can have special prayer time. It is a sacred space to pray, meditate, and hear God speak.) The Youth Minister and the Assistant Youth Minister found the young lady there. They called the ambulance, and the young girl was ok.

We prayed, and I left. I was reflecting on the way home. This was a huge parish. It was in a very nice place. The people were very well off monetarily. Years prior to my getting into Youth Ministry as a Catholic, I would've never thought that young people who had so much would think of things like that. Again, this was years prior to my doing Youth Ministry as a Catholic. I thought that the most they could've been going through was some guy/girl problems. I was wrong. My first years in professional Catholic Youth Ministry were an eye opener. (A side note—If you are, or know someone who is going through this, please speak up and get help. There are plenty who want to help).

Yes, this is an extreme example. I definitely understand this. I've gone back and forth if I should even add this. I didn't have it in the first edit. However, it illustrates that there are plenty, who even if they look like they are ok on the outside, who need and are searching for the love of Christ. This is where the rest of us step in. We have to have the life of the Spirit to help all.

Your situation may not be as extreme by far. It may be something like not understanding your parents, pressure to perform in sports, pressure from parents, etc. Whatever is your case, Christ is for you. His love and purpose is for all! Even if your life is exactly the way you've always dreamed and nothing is wrong at all. You might've had Communion for breakfast and float when you read this. I'm joking again...However, if you can float and bilocate, please let me know! Regardless of your situation, good or bad, you have to know that God is for you and there is a world around you that needs what you have, the love of Christ.

Challenge

Yes, God calls us to go into the world to be "great" because He is great. But let's not forget that God became a man to show what love is. In other words, He humbled himself and showed day-to-day acts of love. Christ's ministry "begins" when He is 30-33 years of age. What did he do before then? He learned. He helped. He cried. He showed that love is first learned through day-to-day activities. This is how we show who God is. This is how we change the world.

Mother Teresa is quoted as saying that if you want to change the world, go home and love your family. What she's saying is to start with the people you see every day, and that's how you learn to love and change the world. How do we treat the people right next to us?

It is not only saying to go and stand on a corner and beat someone's head in with a Bible, or at work or at school, although maybe that works in some cases. If this is the case, pray about it and do it. Of course, do not beat anyone over the head with anything…except the enemy. (I'm *half*-joking.) But it also means to simply love and be firm, that regardless of what God calls you to do, you are called to be faithful right there.

You first recognize your relationship with the

Spirit, then you start living in love right where you are. That means some of you should put this book down and go tell your wife, your mother, your father, your children, your family that you love them. That means for some that you should pick up a phone and say I'm sorry.

That means you stop and get on your knees and ask God to bring a face to mind, bring an instance to mind, bring people to mind that you need to pray for and for whom you need to be the light of Christ now! It takes patience. It takes time. It takes being bold! That's what St. Augustine did, and that's what Mary did. Their call is our call. Their mandate is the same for all Christians in the world who are walking with Christ and have life in the Spirit: "Go!..Go!...Go!.. and be bold with who we serve."

Be bold with who loves you and loves all those around you. Be bold with the Creator of your soul. Because when you do so, life makes more sense. When you look outside you see that this world needs something and this causes you to look inside of you. Notice that the little "voice" in the back of your "mind" telling you "I love you and I am here, now go and be bold" is the Holy Spirit letting you know that you belong to the God of all!

Chapter Four

Heart Felt

J Cole, "Kevin's Heart"

Because I'm the way that I am, I get asked frequently who are my favorite "new" artists. You see, there's a huge distinction between hip hop artists today and artists of "yesterday." The much newer artists that are really famous today tend to rap about the things you would think about when glorifying a "hip hop lifestyle." I'm very aware of all these and what's trending, but I've always been drawn to artists who were somewhat deep thinkers and some who even talked about God a lot. I know that may sound odd to some, but believe it or not there is a whole "secular" side that did both from the beginning.

Artists like Poor Righteous Teachers, Brand Nubian, De La Soul, Jungle Brothers, X-Clan, etc. These are just a few. True some aspects of these songs were negative, but a lot of it was very positive, at least in the world I grew up in. They spoke of uplifting the human person. How "the god in you" makes you righteous and to never forget that. They even talked about the responsibility that we have to give back to the community and to uplift those around us. I know that's weird for a lot of you to hear and grasp, but it's in there.

With that as my foundation, it is no doubt that I tend to gravitate (on the "secular" side) to artists like Kendrick Lamar, who just won a Pulitzer Prize for one of his albums that is a classic. He dances between topics and problems of the world today and shows how each of them lead to something more…God. He even has a track labeled "God." However, he is not the only one that I know is really good ("dope" in our colloquialism") and has some good content. Another is J Cole.

J Cole reminds me a lot of the people I used to listen to and even hang around. He is from Fayetteville, NC. One of his most famous albums, that will go down as a classic, is about his hometown. What's funny is I lived in Fayetteville for 3 years during my middle to some of my high school years. I even know about the parts of the city that he raps about. But this is not the only reason why I like him by far. On one of his latest albums he raps about an incident that was really big in the pop culture here in the US a few years ago. A very well-known celebrity, Kevin Hart, was caught cheating on his wife. Kevin Hart got on social media crying and apologizing about the incident. J Cole wrote a song about it from Kevin's point of view, available on YouTube at https://youtu.be/EixT3caIuxM. The artist declares his love for his wife and his desire to keep her, confessing his selfishness and the kind of pain it might cause.

Kevin realized that cheating on his significant other was wrong, and the track expresses how he could not get over it. He is rapping to his wife, at the time, about what he did and how much it hurts. He's showing that he's selfish, egotistic, and pretending to be happy when he's around his family. In other words, the whole time he's rapping and doing this, he recognizes that his heart is not where it should be. The outside actions of what led him to evaluate his "inner self" and what he sees does not make him happy. The world on the outside was taken "in," and now he is full of remorse. The track shows that his "heart" is wrong and selfish. It is profound about the results of sin and our narcissistic culture and our US world. The actions of a faulty, selfish "love" made J Cole speak of "Kevin's Heart."

This is the exact opposite of how Luke portrays

Mary and how real love is in her heart. Let's turn there to see our Mother's heart.

Luke's Look at Mary's heart

Luke gives little "hints" of how Mary reacts to real love in the world around her. He is often referring to the beginning of his "good news," "But Mary kept all these things, pondering them in her heart" (Luke 2:19). Again, He went down with them and came to Nazareth, and was obedient to them; and His mother kept all these things in her heart" (Luke 2:51).

Luke is making a point from the beginning. He just went through how the Holy Spirit will overshadow Mary, and because of that deep relationship that Mary has with the Holy Spirit, with God, Jesus will be the result. In a way, he is now saying that because of that deep relationship now when she sees Jesus' actions in the world, instead of simply reacting, instead of taking it just like another day of simple actions in the world, she let these actions become a part of her. She saw God. She saw love moving in the world and knowing that these moments are so special she "soaked in them." She let these actions become more and more of her, and she hid these things within her, in her "heart."

Hildebrand's Look at the "Heart"

To talk about the "heart" in the biblical world is much different from what we may think today whenever we say the word heart. Today, we tend to think of the heart as a part of our body, an organ that pumps blood to the different parts of our bodies. The "heart" of Mary is different from that. The Church recognizes that the "heart" is vitally important to our spiritual growth. "The spiritual tradition of the Church also emphasizes the heart, in the biblical sense of the depths of one's being, where the person decides for or against God" (CCC, 368). It is the place from where we decide things. What things? The things from this world, everything, but especially things that have to do with God.

The heart is the very center of the person, something one often overlooks. The heart is a primary source of all intentions. When I was in graduate school I came across someone's writings that I "loved." He influenced me more than I realized. He helped me put into words things that were hard for me. One of these is the "heart."

Our culture talks about the "heart" quite a bit. Look at just one of the songs that I randomly picked at the beginning. It even recognizes that the actions of this world affect the heart. *The Catechism of the Catholic Church* quotes the New Testament: "For out of the heart come evil thoughts, murder, adultery, fornication, theft, false witness, slander. These are what defile a man" (Matthew 15:19-20). But in the heart also resides charity, the source of the good and pure works, which sin wounds" (CCC 1853). One must come to the understanding of how important our heart is.

One of my favorite philosophers (for those non-academics—a really smart dude) of all time, Dietrich Von Hildebrand, wrote a lot about "The Heart." I first came across his work during my studies for my graduate degree in Theology and really got to know him through reading some of his work during my studies for my graduate degree in Philosophy. It's there where I realized that "the Heart" is so much more than what we normally think.

"In order to understand the nature of the heart, we must realize that in many respects the heart is more the real self of the person than his intellect and his will"(Dietrich Von Hildebrand, *The Heart* (South Bend, Indiana: Augustine Press, 1965), 67). Side Note—I'm about to really "nerd out" here, in my way, and go really deep here. So, just read and bear with me.

You'll see why in a second.

The heart is a sort of modern thing that people write about. Do not get me wrong. We have always written about it in one way or another, but it is not until about the 20th Century that we started really going into what it really is. Dr. Ronda Chervin, a dear sweet lady and friend whom I look up to, a disciple of that philosopher, Dietrich Von Hildebrand, who has written many books herself and been on EWTN (a famous Catholic Television station) countless times, states, "The intellect and the will play a vital part in the person, as far as decisions and other things that the person does. But, most thinkers over-emphasize 'the intellect and the will' over the heart because of false ideas about emotions." Translation—we write and talk about the will and intellect a lot and we need to, but we sort of overdue it because we really do not know what emotions are and how they play out in love.

An example that Dr. Chervin often gives to bring out this point is the parent who manifests great love for the family by working hard, often at jobs he or she doesn't like very much. However, if that same parent never expresses delight in the children from the heart, they may still feel unloved!

Love without emotions is robotic. Love with only

emotions is dramatic, stalker-ish, and sometimes just gets weird like the Netflix show "You"! All you need to do is look at most "chick flicks." Focusing on our emotions only is being "unstable." Think about how many times our emotions change during the day....a lot. I woke up happy. Something happened about 10 minutes into the day that made me mad, etc. We can all do this. Emotions change. This is why we need the intellect and will. These are the things that help "balance" our emotions, in this case the "heart."

Trying to love with only the intellect and will is cold. It leaves the concept of love as something that we have just simply "will" to do. I "will" to love my wife. I "will" to love my kids. That's right in one sense. But I LOVE romance also! I love "heartfelt" moments with my kids. These are because of emotions, and all of it is in the "heart."

Feeling down or tired is not fully in one's direct control, and sometimes we give into irrational feelings of rage or despair due to so many things around us and in us. However, joy, hope, gratitude, and authentic love are all feelings in our heart.

Betrothed Love

The heart is the most intimate and the most authentic part of the person. It is much more than the emoji that you send "bae." It is the deep part of the person that many have tried to define through the years.

True love is a voice of the heart and allows us to say, and really believe, that we love a person and long for a return of their love. It's the heart of the other person which one wants to call our own. It is not the kind of love that is filled with the modern "romance" novels or "chick-flicks." It is "authentic love."

As Dietrich Von Hildebrand puts it: "The lover wants to pour his love into the heart of the beloved, he wants to affect his heart, to fill it with happiness; and only then will he feel that he has really reached the beloved, his very self." (Dietrich Von Hildebrand, The Heart, 67). Isn't that beautiful!

In marriage, betrothed love, you really want your most precious part of you to fully look at the other and "give all" of you to the other. This is why marriage is so much more than a contract; it's a covenant. It's a bond that is unbreakable. It's bound together by God and in God. It is a fully given openness to the other person, without fear of being hurt. That is what it was designed to be from the beginning. I know this is so different than what we're used to hearing in the American culture. However, just keep reading!

This is what Adam and Eve did, when Adam looks at Eve and claims, "Behold flesh of my flesh"(Gen 2). In a way he is saying this same thing. You are my flesh. You are me. I am you. We are one, and we "connect" on a whole other level than Adam did with the animals. It is a mutual giving of the other bound together by something bigger than themselves, God. We connect in God, and because God knows us more deeply than we know ourselves, God unites us more deeply than we can even explain, and all of this is in our "heart." Isn't his statement a full of expression of what we really feel and know when we truly fall in love? This expresses the heart as the very center of our being.

The goal of all human knowing and willing is happiness. But, to truly answer the question: Is a man truly happy? one cannot answer with: if he wills it, or if he uses his intellect then he can be happy. No, this is false. It is in the heart alone that true happiness is attained. Happiness is a gift, a grace from God. It is "like dew upon our heart, shining gratuitously like a sunray into our soul (Dietrich Von Hildebrand, *The*

Heart, 69). One can will and try to use one's brain power to try to reach true happiness, but in most aspects it would really be pointless. The same could be said for all true meaningful human experiences: tears, deep love, "being moved," true charity, etc. These are all gifts from above. These all come from the very depths of the person's soul: "the heart."

Maybe you are wondering how in the world we would go from a love of a parent to love of a spouse. Well, first the Church is the "Body of Christ" (Romans 12:4-5; 1 Corinthians 12:12-27; Ephesians 1:22-23; Ephesians 4:12; Colossians 1:24). And Our Lord, Jesus is the "head of the body, the church" (Colossians 1:18).

St. Paul explains this physical relationship and divine spiritual relationship in Ephesians 5:22-33:

"Wives, submit to your own husbands, as to the Lord. For the husband is head of the wife, as also Christ is head of the church; and He is the Savior of the body. Therefore, just as the church is subject to Christ, so let the wives be to their own husbands in everything.

"Husbands, love your wives, just as Christ also loved the church and gave Himself for her, that He might sanctify and cleanse her with the washing of water by the word, that He might present her to Himself a glorious church, not having spot or wrinkle or any such thing, but that she should be holy and without blemish."

In short, husbands are called to love their own wives as their own bodies. Sit with that if you've ever thought about marriage. We, men, are called to love as "Christ Loved the Church." How did Christ love the Church? He died for her. Yeah. That's deep. This means that we (the church) are called to love Christ almost like a spouse but deeper. All this is why you can use marriage (love of spouse) to how a parent loves, because Scripture does it....

Back to Momma Mary

Take all of that "talk" about "the heart." We see that when Momma Mary ponders the actions and movements of God, they affect her in a way that is hard to describe, but very beautiful. Her "heart" is full of grace. So, in other words, she loves perfectly. She loves Jesus perfectly and loves us perfectly. Just as all amazing mothers do. She knows that when we come to her and talk (pray), we are showing our deep admiration in our own hearts for her Son, Our Lord. This is beautiful! And because her "heart" is so in tune with God, she knows how to respond. She knows how to react. She knows that the pain we feel is like what she went through when seeing Her son on the Cross. She knows what pain and turmoil are.

How many of us could watch our own children, or someone we love be tortured, dragged through the streets and hung in front of everyone? I have children, and I can only imagine how that would feel. She does. So, when we come before her and bring our questions, our wants, our needs, she is answering from a depth of her soul that is full of true love. She's answering from her "heart" because she is a true mother, and good mothers feel for their children.

Us

We've all seen the movements of mothers' hearts or our caregiver's hearts throughout our lives. If you're a teen, you can probably remember when you would fall and your mother would help you. Or, if your mother was not there, the person who took care of you. However, if you're of Latino descent you know you would hear "sana colita, sana colita, sana colita de ran…" and then a lot of Vicks would be put on you! LOL! Yeaaaaa, the good old days! Oh, and I really do think that Vicks works. It's in the Bible, somewhere in

Second Opinions. I'm joking again, of course...

Anyway, when your mother or caregiver would pick you up, do you remember their look? Or how about when you were sick? (again, after the Vicks). I've seen my wife sleep on the floor of the room where our sons slept when they got sick. I remember when I first noticed it with my first son. I asked why in the world would she need to sleep on the floor? Her response was, because that's what mothers do to make sure they're ok through the night. She said it like it was nothing. Yeaa... she's a living saint.

If you're a young adult, do you remember when you graduated from high school or college, and do you remember your mother's/caregiver's face? Do you remember what she/they said? Do you remember the different things that went on in your life and she/they was/were there rooting you on? I've seen my wife go to every play, every award, every little part of my sons' lives regardless of what it was. I've even seen her stomach get upset because our son might be feeling anxious (like on the first day of school). I've seen her always sacrifice herself over and over for our boys. I've asked her time and time again, why do you do that? She responds like nothing, "that's what mother's do."

Yes, that is what mother's do. Even if you did not

have a mother who was there, this is all the more reason for a spiritual mother. A mother who ponders these things in her heart. This is why Mary is so important. Mothers who love ponder all the things in their hearts, as we all should.

Hey, if you're reading this stop and call or go tell your mother how much you appreciate her and love her. It will mean a lot because she has "pondered [your life] in her heart." She knows the inner part of her loves all her children. If she does that, how much more does Mary do that with Jesus and for us? You see, Mary's love for us is based in her love for her Son, Our Lord. Her love is so graceful because she is in touch with the Holy Spirit and knows Jesus personally.

After you get done talking with your mother, talk with your other mother, Mary. She loves you because she has "pondered all these things in her heart." This allowed her to know Jesus in a different way. We should do the same. After you talk/pray with Mary, pick up your Bible and read through Luke 1 and "ponder" the things in your heart. See how it changes your perspective on Mary, on Jesus, and on you. You'll be surprised.

Chapter Five

The Strength of Our Lady(ies)

Lecrae, "All I Need is You"

I just realized that all of the tracks that I have been referring to are "secular." This is "Christian-eze" language. For those who don't know, the word "secular" is used by religious people to describe things that are not labeled specifically Christian. Gospel music, worship music, etc., are labeled Christian. But anything that is not overtly Christian is labeled secular. Side Note—does that include the "Happy Birthday" song we all sing? Or what about a song that is on a commercial? These are not specifically Christian but technically are labeled "secular."

Yeaahhhh, it gives me a headache, also. I sometimes think we worry about labels too much in our culture. Labels are important but, in this case, it only boxes the subject in. It can put parameters as to where God can be seen and heard. For those complaining, just read and sit with Psalm 24, especially verse 1. But, this is a subject for a different book. Back to what I was saying…using "secular" vs. non-secular. This leads me to someone whom I almost look up to. He has pushed me to define myself as a better Christian man and father and how I express that in the culture I was brought up in…hip hop.

This person is Lecrae. I don't want to get too much into his background, but there are a lot of similarities. He has been married for a number of years, and he somewhat recently released a song that really helped him "reach" (pun intended—if you know of Lecrae's music you would know why I use that word – find it on YouTube at https://youtu.be/-5gcX3sIoUs) a different crowd from what he normally would about his wife. When I first heard it, I honestly felt it. Everything he was saying, I think any man who has been married and who has gone through things would say. The artist explains in "All I need is you" that all he needs is his girl by his side.

In this track, Lecrae is stating that in this life he needs his wife. Right, I hear you. "Dr. G. all we need is God! We do not need anyone else." To this I respond with, "Yesssirrr. But trust me, if you had a woman like Lecrae is talking about you would really understand what he's saying." You see, he is talking about that simple theological principle that we are made in God's image (Gen 1:26). Because of such, we are made for others. According to Gods plan, we see that special bond of man and woman before the fall in Genesis 3. I would love to say that is what he's getting at! I know that's how I look at my wife. My wife and I have been married for 20 years, and I can honestly say this. I would not be the man I am without her. Yes, I would not be the person I am without my relationship with God. However, I do believe that God has given me her to know Him more. I believe God had blessed me with a woman so that I can honestly be all I am, open and transparent, and she the same and because we do this we each know God better. So, in a way by knowing her more I know God more because we are in God.

So, when Lecrae is singing all he needs is her, what he's really saying is all he needs is the God that is in her, the God that blessed him with her, and that lets him know God more by knowing her more. This is what Christian love is, in a way, knowing others deeply to know God more. Knowing the created being to know the Creator more. Knowing the woman (or man) points to the Creator because the Creator knows you and the woman (or man) deeper than we know ourselves. This is how Mary is. By knowing Mary, we know God and we need that! We need her strength!

Who is the Woman?

The book of Revelation is pretty "scary." I've heard this over and over, both as a non-Catholic Christian and as a Catholic. I think it's mainly because we are "scared" of what's unfamiliar to us, and we have heard so many things about the Book of Revelation that we really think we know everything about it. That is how I used to be.

When I was non-Catholic Christian it seemed like the majority of my studies were about the Book of Revelation. I would study it. Read books on it. Watch movies on it. I wanted to know the "Anti-Christ" (though that phrase is NOT in the Book of Revelation at all). I wanted to know who would the "Beast" be and was. I wanted to know all of that, and prior to my conversion to the Catholic faith, I would've stated that I knew a lot about the Book of Revelation.

Let me harken back to the time when my brother-in-law had just converted to the Catholic faith. I knew that he was a "baby-Christian," so I was sure that he was "tricked" into thinking Catholicism was a real

Christian religion. I mean, after all, these guys do NOT even read the Bible. That is what I used to think.

One day a good friend of mine, a Protestant Pastor, was like, "Let's trip him up. Let's do a Bible Study with him and show him how false the Catholic Faith is!" We were even going to do the "hardest" book, the Book of Revelation. We called him up and he responded with a huge YES. We were excited. We knew we were going to get him and get him good about being Catholic.

We met a few times, and I really felt we were starting to get to him. We would have differences interpreting Scripture, but that is a norm in the non-Catholic world. The Book of Revelation is definitely one of those books where you can hold to different interpretations and still believe in the same God, etc. So, we get to the Book of Revelation chapter 12. "And a great portent appeared in heaven, a woman clothed with the sun, with the moon under her feet, and on her head a crown of twelve stars; she was with child and she cried out in her pangs of birth, in anguish for delivery." I remember this very vividly. Very calm and collected, he asked one question: "Who is the woman?"

My response was, of course, it's the Church bro! Or something like that. He asked again, "Yes, but who is the woman actually?" It has to be someone. If we look and see the other portions of the Book of Revelation, "the Son of Man" is Jesus. The beast who rises up is the Enemy. Then who is the actual woman? He added that the actual numbers of the chapters and verses in the Bible were added by monks. He left it at that. I knew he was right about the numbers part. I still couldn't answer who the woman was. Hmmm. I remember thinking I need to look at this, and I did.

Let's all of us now take a look at the woman of the Book of Revelations together. This is the end of Revelation 11:19,

"Then God's temple in heaven was opened, and the ark of his covenant was seen within his temple; and there were flashes of lightning, loud noises, peals of thunder, an earthquake, and heavy hail....12 And a great portent appeared in heaven, a woman clothed with the sun, with the moon under her feet, and on her head a crown of twelve stars; she was with child and she cried out in her pangs of birth, in anguish for delivery."

To continue our exploration, we need to look at another theme in Scripture: the Ark.

The Ark

All through pop culture, theories of the Ark, what

it looks like, where it is, can be found. But don't stop there please. If we're going to be honest and look at the Ark, some context has to be found. In other words, we have to make sure we're reading this right, so we need to look at some history and so forth to understand that when the Book of Revelation states "the Ark," we know what it's referring to.

The author of the Book of Revelation, besides the Holy Spirit, is John. John is in prison. He's "locked up," and he cannot worship (Revelation 1). It's "the Lord's Day," which is Sunday by Christian tradition. So, God allows John to see how worship is done in heaven. When we get to Chapter 11, God's temple in heaven is opened. It's more than that though. God allows John to see the ark of the Covenant. Now, if you know anything about the Bible, you would automatically go back to the Israelites in the wilderness. They carried the Ark of the Covenant around with them while in the Desert and when they built the temple, the Ark of the Covenant was placed there.

If you look at 1 Chronicles 28:2, Psalm 99:5; 132:7-8, etc., you will see that the Ark was REALLY important. It was almost the most important symbol of God's being with His people because that's where He would meet them. The Mercy Seat was where God would dwell. He said, "There, above the cover between the two cherubim that are over the ark of the covenant law, I will meet with you and give you all my commands for the Israelites" (Exodus 25:22). It was even carried into battle by the Israelites because it meant that God was fighting for them. In Joshua 6, in order for the walls of Jericho to fall, they carried it around the walls seven times with them.

The top or cover of the Ark was called the "mercy seat." This is where the high priest would sprinkle the atoning blood for Israel's sins one time a year. In 2 Kings 25, when Babylon conquered Jerusalem and trashed the temple, the Ark was seen the last time. 2 Maccabees 2:4-8 says that the ark is in a cave on Mount Nebo where it would remain until, "God gathers his people together again..." When John sees the Ark, it would automatically signify that this is the time fulfilled in the Old Testament. This was the time that "God would meet His people."

I found out something while I was looking into this. Did you know that at the Mass readings on the Visitation of the Blessed Virgin Mary (August 22), the text from 1 Chronicles 13:14 is read, "The ark of God remained in the house of Obed-edom with his family for three months, and the LORD blessed Obed-edom's household and all that he possessed" (1 Chronicles 13:14). I found out and asked myself, why? Why would Catholics read about the Ark when celebrating Mary?

He-Brews

The book of Hebrews was written by a high scholar who knew theology. (I'm obviously making the situation as if it were in modern days.) Some say it's not St. Paul. I believe it was. He knew his stuff. He was a trained theologian and knew how to address people. Whatever you believe, we have to say that Hebrews was written by someone who knew his faith and was preaching to people who knew their faith, likely priests. Why is that important? Well, we find out what was in the Ark of the Covenant in the book of Hebrews. "Behind the second curtain was a room called the Most Holy Place, which had the golden altar of incense and the gold-covered ark of the covenant. This ark contained the gold jar of manna, Aaron's staff that had budded, and the stone tablets of the covenant" (Hebrews 9:4).

The *Catechism of the Catholic Church* speaks to this point: "Christians therefore read the Old Testament in the light of Christ crucified and risen.

Such typological reading discloses the inexhaustible content of the Old Testament; but it must not make us forget that the Old Testament retains its own intrinsic value as Revelation reaffirmed by our Lord himself. Besides, the New Testament has to be read in the light of the Old. Early Christian catechesis made constant use of the Old Testament. As an old saying put it, the New Testament lies hidden in the Old and the Old Testament is unveiled in the New."(CCC 129)

What it's stating is that what we see in the Old Testament is fulfilled in the New Testament. Apply this to the items in the Ark. The Manna in the Old Testament is Jesus in the New Testament (John 6:58, etc.). The Staff of Aaron, if you know the story, is about who was the priest that God wanted (in Numbers 17). The Old Testament finds its fulfillment in Jesus (Hebrews 4:14-16). The "stone tablets of the covenant" is really the Law, the Ten Commandments in the Old Testament (Exodus 20). Jesus is the fulfillment of the law (Matthew 5 :17). Can you see that each of the items in the Ark are fulfilled in Jesus?

What is better, the thing represented or the thing that it's supposed to represent? Another way, what is better, the Ten Commandments or Jesus? If you're a Christian, obviously the answer is Jesus. Ok, if the Ark of the Covenant in the Old Testament had to be perfectly made in Exodus 37 and was so holy that if anyone who touched it and was not supposed to would die (1 Samuel 6:19), why wouldn't the thing that is better be held to that same standard? In other words, if the Ark of the Covenant in the Old Testament had to be perfect with items that only represented Jesus, why wouldn't the "vessel," the womb that God chose to use that fulfilled those items, also have to be perfect? The answer is that it would. The law must be fulfilled, not done away with (Matthew 5:17). That New Testament Ark is Mary's womb. This is one of the reasons the Church labels her the "Ark of the Covenant."

In the Stars

Revelation 11 is about the Ark, and Revelation 12 picks up with a woman. Bear in mind that it was only in medieval times that the numbers were added and chapters were made in the Bible. What if the separation of Revelation 11 and 12 only hinders what is so obvious when you put them together? The Ark of Revelation 11 is the woman at the beginning of Revelation 12 and this woman has strength, more than we realize.

" And a great portent appeared in heaven, a woman clothed with the sun, with the moon under her feet, and on her head a crown of twelve stars; she was with child and she cried out in her pangs of birth, in anguish for delivery. And another portent appeared in heaven; behold, a great red dragon, with seven heads and ten horns, and seven diadems upon his heads. His tail swept down a third of the stars of heaven, and cast them to the earth. And the dragon stood before the woman who was about to bear a child, that he might devour her child when she brought it forth." (Revelation 12:1-3).

A Picture is Worth a 1000k Words

Have you ever looked at a drawing or a painting? Of course you have! You even see them on Instagram or Snapchat. They're amazing. They say that these come from a deep part of our psyche. In other words, a picture is a part of us. It is in the inner part of who we are. That's amazing, especially when it comes to something we have seen over and over. I know I've seen it way before I was Catholic, way before I was Christian. There is a common picture, or the big word for this is "iconography" or religious art of Mary. In it, a woman dressed in blue and white is standing on top of the moon or world, surrounded by the sun, with the moon at her feet. She has a crown made of stars. This is something I've noticed all around the world. I had no idea that it was Revelation 11 and 12!

You see, John sees this woman, "a great sign in the sky." If you read closely, you really see that John is going back to Genesis 37:7-10. This is where the image seen then represents Joseph's father, mother, and brothers, the patriarchs, and the twelve tribes of Israel. Another way of looking at it is the woman represents Israel (Ps 87, Is 66:8-11). N. T. Write states, "She represents the entire story of God's people, chosen to carry forward his plans..." In other words, she is carrying the church, all of us. She is our mother. However, there's more.

I don't see the next part in these pictures, which is why I actually picture Mary much differently than the majority of pictures we've seen. We seem to forget that there is a huge red dragon there!

Now that we have established the Ark is Mary, picture Mary in front of a 7-headed dragon. Let's take it a step deeper. Picture PREGNANT Mary in front of a 7-headed red dragon. Let's take another step. Picture a little 13-14 year old Middle-Eastern girl in front of a

7-headed, red dragon with sharp teeth, breathing fire. The dragon is towering over little Mary. How do you picture Mary looking back up at the beast? I'm sure some would say scared. How would you be in front of a creature like that? If you're honest, you would be scared and probably praying.... a lot. Do you picture Mary like that? I do not. I picture her like the women in my family, who are fighters. I don't mean metaphorically, although that's also true. But, I mean physically. The women I know and knew, the ones in my house that I grew up with were strong and fighters!

My world

School

Growing up, it was usual to see fights both in school and out of school. It was a norm to see guys fighting guys, females fighting females and, yes, females fighting guys. You probably had to go back to read that again. Yes, that was actually normal, to see females fist fight each other and males. If you grew up like I did, you'd understand. They would put Vaseline on their faces, earrings (usually the really big ones), and fist fight. Yes, pulling hair, but really fist fighting. My sisters were like this, also.

This is how I picture Mary. She is a fighter. She's standing there pregnant but with her fists up facing the creature, almost like a Mixed Martial Artist (MMA) combined with a girl on the block breaking out the Vaseline, combined with a fierce tone of a parent protecting her child from death. That's how I picture her, a mother who is protecting her child in the midst of danger. And if you think about it, isn't that what good mothers do? And isn't that what we need, a spiritual mother fighting for us? I know you might not get that but wait. Keep reading.

As I was writing this, a mother came into my office at the school where I work. She wanted to talk about her son. She was worried about him and asked for some perspective. I pointed her to Mary. I find myself doing that a lot. If you're a dude reading this, there's a lot we can learn from her, especially her strength. I cannot tell you how many times this has happened through the years. Mother's and father's coming in, shedding tears, fighting for their sons and daughters. They each know that it's their responsibility. They each know that whatever they do will affect their child in a way that no one else can. I point them to Mary because she's the prime example of how to fight for her children in the face of danger. If you think about it, it's somewhat embedded in female nature to fight and go through hardship for their child at all costs. Ok, I'm exaggerating, you say? Wait. Keep reading and you'll see.

Birth

Years ago, right before we had our first son, I was excited to be at the birth. My friends were hyping me up. They told me it was going to be the most beautiful thing I've ever experienced. They told me how deep the moment was and to make sure I'm there for the actual birth because it is amazing. So, I was excited. I knew that the moment things happened I would be there to see everything…and I was.

The day came. We were at the hospital. They took my beautiful wife behind closed doors, and it was finally time. I got dressed in the scrubs and prepared to enter the room. They walked me through the halls and into the operating room. It was a build-up. The lights. The cold room. The scrubs. The doctor and nurses. It was happening. I slowly opened the door. My wife was having a C-section. And I saw everything…and I mean everything.

If you've ever seen the board game "Operation" you will know what I saw. Yeah. It was not what I expected. Now it gets even more interesting. My wife, laying on the table with everything in the wide open, quickly popped her head out from behind the veil (again, the veil did not allow her to look down. So, she had no idea what I could see). She pops her head out and with a big smile says, "Hey, Baby!" As if everything was normal and her day was the best day possible.

I stood there like, broooo is this happening?!!?! She was laying down prepared to have our son, C-Section, and a veil was placed just below her neck to where she could not tell what was happening. Her head popped from behind that veil, smiling and she says, "Hey, Baby." Yeah. I was a little shaken.

It was funny, but they were right. It was beautiful. It was mystical. I remember holding my son and looking down at him. I remember my wife's face, in spite of everything below her neck being wide open, smiling, a smile that more than shined. It more than radiated true beauty. It was a smile from heaven, from God. It was a perfect picture of love and sacrifice. I'm tearing up thinking about it, and it was about 20 years ago. It still takes me back. It still lets me know that there is "beauty in the struggle." (as JCole would state). It still lets me know what St. Paul says in Romans 1:20—"For since the creation of the world God's invisible qualities – his eternal power and divine nature – have been clearly seen, being understood from what has been made." God is in the very creation of our being, and he uses women as a reminder of it. It's been that way always, if we stop and look. It's been that way since the beginning.

There is a strength in women that I have seen over and over through the years. Oh, yeah, when we were released from the hospital my wife refused to take any pain medicine. After a C-Section and their sending us home a few short days after, she took NO pain medicine. I remember pleading with her to take it because I could tell she was in pain. She said no. Why, you might ask. Because she was breastfeeding and didn't want our son to have any of that in his system. Yeah. She sacrificed for our son. I have to add here— that could NOT be me. (By the way, if you do not know what a C-Section is, you might want to look it up. It'll paint the picture better.)

After everything, she said she would absolutely do it again. And, of course, we do have two more boys. I'm honest, and I know God is working for me, but that really couldn't be me. First, I would've asked for the

Doc to prescribe pretty much anything to take the pain away…heroin included. I'm joking, of course! But, I definitely would've taken the pain medicine. I think a lot of men would. Which leads me to the second point. I don't know how many men would continue to give life if it was up to us. We whine when we get sick. We need help! LOL. I'm half joking of course. But, it's true, there is a strength intrinsically woven into the very nature of women that makes them say yes over and over regardless of the pain, regardless of their own situation…why? Because they love. That's it, no more, no less!

Women have something that we all need. There is a strength in them for their children, us, that allows humanity to go on. I've learned so much from my wife. This is one of the basic things: women are strong. Really strong. Which leads me to a question, if women are so strong and they are physical, visible to us, then how much more strong is our mommy Mary who is not physically on earth but an embodied spirit in heaven? We need our mothers for life now. We need our mother Mary for life, also. Just like in the Book of Revelation, she stands in front of the 7-headed dragon, protecting her offspring—her child is the same way she stands in front of the Enemy (7-headed dragon) now and protects and fights for us as a real spiritual mother should!

If you stop and think about it, this draws a different picture than what we're used to thinking about Mary. In this case, I do not see her "meek and mild," but rather firm and strong. I see her standing there in a fighting stance willing to go through any type of pain for her children, us the Church. That's a mother. That's Our Mother. Why? Because that's what all good mothers do.

Challenge

If you're reading this, stop and pray. Read the end of Revelation 11 and the beginning of Revelation 12. Stop and picture the Enemy. Now stop and picture Mary facing the Enemy protecting her children, us! Imagine yourself feeling safe there while she is practically shielding you from the Enemy. Imagine her there fighting for you. Imagine her hair, her hands, her eyes. Imagine her looking at the Enemy assured that she will do anything and everything to protect her children. It's different. It's beautiful. It's Mary, and I love her with everything. She's my mommy! Yeah, I'm a Momma's Boy....and proud of it!

Closing

We've come a long way, and it's only the beginning. What you just read is simply a collection of thoughts, insights, findings, and explanations about someone dear to me, Momma Mary. Mary is a really hard subject for some of us. She was really hard for me because I didn't understand so much as a child growing up. I didn't get why people "adored" her (so I thought). I didn't understand the rosary. I didn't understand the statues in the corner of my abuela's houses. I didn't understand the little cards with a fair-skinned beautiful woman on them. I didn't understand the blue hood this woman wore. I didn't understand her Son. I didn't understand what a relationship with God was. I didn't understand church language. I didn't understand a lot…I can keep going. I think you get the picture.

However, when you're a child, you don't have to understand a lot, but you do trust. My trust as a child with Mary began about 12 or so years ago. I never heard of Mary as the Mother of God, the Ark of the Covenant, etc. I never even heard of what most of us take for granted all the time in our faith. For me, Mary was just another woman. To me and many who do not understand who Mary is and why she is so important to our faith, she is just someone that God used. He could've used anyone. My response now to that is, Yes, he could've. He is God and can use whomever he chooses. However, he didn't. He chose Mary and Mary chose him. She is the one and only that God chose to use and who said yes to carry Our Lord. Even if we were to stop there, we would have to admit that there is something more than average to Mary! From the very beginning, I knew there was more to her and as I began to study and pray, more became revealed to me about Mary. I hope this is a little something for wherever you're at in your journey of being a faithful Christian/Catholic.

Maybe you're thinking this isn't for you. I would ask you to pray about it. Maybe you're thinking that you wish there were more to know. I would say, pray about it and look. I have a feeling this will not be my only short book on Mary. The more I'm on this journey, the more I keep finding little insights about how her love is revealed. But isn't that what Mothers do? They let their children grow and, as they grow, they give them more and more, to where eventually the child is an adult living in a deep relationship with them? The same is true of Mary, and what's even better she wants you to know and see Jesus the way she does. It's really not even about her. It's about her son, Our Lord.

You think you know Jesus? Sit with Mary, let her tell you and show you how to love. Let her show you how to live in a relationship with her son. That's what this is all about. She says, "Do whatever he [Jesus] tells you…" in Jesus' first Miracle at Cana in John 2:5. When you sit with her, you realize she tells us the same thing, "Do whatever he tells you…" This is the basic Christian call. This is our call. This is living….

Hail Mary….

Notes on Mary

(Use these blank pages to jot down some thoughts on how this book has spoken to you. Then, share this book with someone.)

Notes on Mary

Notes on Mary

Notes on Mary